exploring

HEAVENLY PLACES

INVESTIGATING DIMENSIONS OF HEALING

VOLUME 1

BY

Paul L Cox

Barbara Kain Parker

EXPLORING HEAVENLY PLACES, VOLUME 1
Investigating Dimensions of Healing

By Paul L Cox and Barbara Kain Parker

Aslan's Place Publications
9315 Sagebrush Street
Apple Valley, CA 92308
760-810-0990
www.aslansplace.com

Unless otherwise indicated, scriptures are taken from the:
New King James Version (NKJV): New King James Version®. Copyright © 1982 by Thomas Nelson. Used by permission. All rights reserved.

Scripture taken from HOLY BIBLE, NEW INTERNATIOANL VERSION ®. Copyright © 1973, 1978, 1984, 2010, 2011 by International Bible Society. Used by permission of Zondervan. All rights reserved.

Scripture quotations marked YOUNG'S are from Young's Literal Translations by Robert Young, 1989. Reprinted by Baker Book House, Grand Rapids, Michigan, copyright © 2003.

TABLE OF CONTENTS

INTRODUCTION TO THE EXPLORING HEAVENLY PLACES SERIES

I (Paul) had settled into my seat at the morning worship service of a Washington D.C. church but was startled when, well into his message, the pastor said, "You know, we really do make things more complicated then they need to be. Everything is really quite simple." I thought, "I do not know if I believe that." After operating in the gift of discernment for more than twenty years, I am now more than convinced than ever that everything really is much more complicated than we think.

Pastors are woefully reluctant to explore the complexities of the spiritual world. We have boiled our sermons down to three, five, or ten points that can be easily projected onto our PowerPoint screens. However, in the midst of the weekly routine of presenting sermons, pastors are confronted with the spiritual, mental, and physical ailments of those we pastor, discovering far too often that we do not have solutions for their pain. On top of that, our own suffering and the suffering of our family members exasperate our angst.

Where is God in all of the hurt? We search for biblical and theological answers, doing our best to tender a response to the questions we are asked. But where are the real tangible answers that result in real relief to genuine pain?

I have not been content to believe there are no answers and contend that there are real complexities of the spiritual world that we have yet to discover. The more we understand the intricacies of the spiritual world, the more precise our prayers become and the more results we will see to our prayers.

I have not arrived at this belief because of my own cleverness but because the Lord keeps revealing more and more to us about the unseen world. As He has taught us, we have seen breakthroughs that were not previously apparent. He has orchestrated each step, taking us from the simple to the more complex; and the deeper our understanding, the more benefits we see for those who long for complete healing.

Exploring Heavenly Places is a new series of books that will explore the amazing and complex world of the spiritual heavenly places that affect our physical world. You will find it most beneficial to first read *Heaven Trek* and *Come Up Higher,* as these books are foundational to the new series. New volumes will continue to be written and added to the series as the Lord directs. Jesus said:

> *But seek first the kingdom of God and His righteousness, and all these things shall be added to you.*[1]

The key is to seek the heavenly places, and then to expect that all we need will be provided.

Long before I wrote *Heaven Trek* and *Come Up Higher,* the Lord revealed the secret of receiving His revelation. Interestingly, that complete revelation did not come to me directly but always developed in the context of other believers. I might first receive a new discernment, have a dream, or be given one word or a phrase; but I never receive full understanding without consulting others. It is in that unity that new revelation is unpacked and understood; it is our journey together that brings enlightenment to the wisdom of the Lord; and it is for this reason that this series will be co-authored with others. I truly believe that it is in unity that the mysteries of the Kingdom will be revealed.

Years ago a man had a vision of me. He described a huge warehouse with several stories, and inside were floor-to-ceiling cubbyhole units like you would see in an old-fashioned post office sorting location. Each of these cubbyholes contained a scroll. He turned to me and said, "All of these scrolls are filled with revelation the Lord wants to show you." I thought, "How can this be as I am already overwhelmed by what He has shown me so far?" Now, over ten years later, I realize that the journey of understanding the marvelous multi-universes of the Lord's creation has just started and there is real hope for those who understand that for those who realize that His desire is for us to be completely healed and released into our generational birthright:

> *The LORD is good and His love endures forever.*[2]

[1] Matthew 6:33
[2] Psalm 100:5; 136:1, NIV

CHAPTER ONE

THE PART IS NOT THE WHOLE

It is often a thought that establishes a wonderful principle in my (Paul) mind—a thought that seems so simple at first that I am tempted just to forget it as a meaningless intrusion into my mind. However, as I am nudged by the Lord to seriously consider the ramifications of that thought, the enormity of the implications can astound me. In such a way, my consciousness was invaded one day in the midst of life's daily routines, "The part is not the whole." Although the thought seemed random, I was not able to ignore or forget it. 'The part is not whole', surfaced again and again, as if my mind was a computer processing a byte of necessary information to solve a complex mathematical equation. And then I understood.

In the fall of 1989, shortly after ministering my first deliverance, a man who had suffered severe childhood abuse approached me indicating that he needed help and felt the Lord had directed him to me for prayer. I was not prepared for what happened next! Suddenly, I was not talking to the man but to a young boy expressing the pain he had suffered. This was my first experience with Multiple Personality Disorder (MPD); and following that ministry session, many others started coming to me who had also experienced terrible pain as young children. I had now been exposed to a psychological world that was both troubling and terrifying.

During the following months I read extensively about MPD and listened to many recorded lectures from experts in the field. As more and more people came for ministry, I started developing a simple understanding of MPD and of the psychological and spiritual complexities of this defense system that is a response to early childhood trauma. Over the years the Lord has fine-tuned my perception of MPD.

1n 1994 the American Psychiatric Association, in its publication of the *Diagnostic and Statistical Manual of Mental Disorders* (DSM-IV), the term 'Multiple Dissociative Disorder' was changed to 'Dissociative Identity Disorder' (DID) in order to more accurately describe the malady. [1] Since those early years, extensive research both by Christians and the academic community has explored the staggering complexities of DID.

In 1998 a mutual friend introduced me to Dr. Tom Hawkins, who had also previously been exposed to DID. He had come to our home for a seven- day visit when we were living on the property of the Center for Prayer Mobilization in Idyllwild, CA. A wonderful friendship developed, and we later spent much more time together and often talked by phone as we matured in our understanding about DID. Tom's ministry, Restoration in Christ Ministries, became a leader in helping those who were severely abused by others. [2]

As I shared in the introduction of the *Exploring Heavenly Places* series, the Lord continues to take us from the simple to the more complex, and this is one example. Even as we learned that a person could be shattered at a young age, we also began to discover that a person could be trapped in places in the ungodly depth, length, width, and height because of lifetime or generational issues. Sometimes this could be explained by our understanding of DID, but not always. As the Lord directed, we noticed that many people who had not been able to receive help before were now noticing dramatic improvement in their lives. It was as if we were exploring many tributaries of a large river, noticing that there seemed to be connections, but unaware of how to reconcile the way they came together amidst all of the revelation we were receiving.

I was often troubled because I could not understand how a person could be trapped in so many different places at one time, and further difficulty surfaced when the person also showed symptoms of DID. How could one function in life on earth and yet inhabit many other places in the spiritual world? As we experienced our own revelation, we noticed that many others were receiving similar truths. Ana Méndez Farrell writes in her book *Regions of Captivity* of ministering to her sister while she was hospitalized. The Lord showed Ana that her sister was trapped in a cave under water, and she provides a visual image of her vision in that book. The Lord revealed to Ana how to minster to her sister and the result was a wonderful healing.

I was astonished because the Lord had also shown many people through dreams and visions that they or others were also trapped under the water. How was this possible? It was clear that Ana could see her sister in the hospital room, yet she also saw her under water. How could she be in two places at one time? It was while looking at Ana's picture that I had a sudden realization my thought, 'The part is not the whole' finally made sense.

A person with DID can have many alter identities (alters), and Dr. Tom Hawkins has given us a good definition of an alter:

> An alter-identity is a completely separated projection of the person's true self, formed through dissociation to enable him to cope in the midst of overwhelming trauma. This is a more accurate designation than alter-personality, as each of these parts has a distinct identity but not always a completely developed personality. They are much more limited in function and awareness than primary identities, which carry the strongest essence of self.[3]

As I have talked to alters, I've noticed that they exhibit the characteristics of a person, sometimes thinking they are the only one in the body. For example, a three-year-old alter may have the memories and personality of a three-year-old; he is everything that a three-year-old is. Yet, the alter is only a part; it is not the entire self. 'The part is not the whole'. The separating of the core identity into alters allows the whole person to be separated into parts that can then be relegated to different places in the spiritual world. Each part has the appearance of the whole, and might even function as a whole; but it is only a part.

We have now learned that the soul and spirit of a person can be separated into parts that can be placed in different locations in time, or in the heavenly realms.

To add to the complexity of this reality, this can happen in the generational line as well and separated generational parts still seem to have influence on a person who is alive today. It is also possible that these parts have been fragmented so that the solution of finding a part and bringing it back to the body is only solved by first bringing the fragments back to the part, at which point the part can be addressed through the Lord's guidance in prayer, returned to the person, and placed into the Lord's perfect time.

In this introductory book we have included articles regarding aspects of the body, soul, and spirit in order to provide a basic understanding of these elements of our humanity and help us see how our beings interact with the unseen. The shattering of these aspects of our lives through wounding prohibits us from becoming all that the Lord wants us to be and enables the enemy to profit from what is rightfully ours. The cure for this pain will be further explored throughout the book series *Exploring Heavenly Places*

[1] http://www.rcm-usa.org/ *Dissociative Identity Disorder: Recognizing and Restoring the Severely Abused* Tom R. Hawkins, Ph.D. "Dissociation is generally considered to be a disturbance or alteration in consciousness, memory, identity or perception of the environment. Normally, a person integrates these various functions, whereas dissociation is a compartmentalization of these functions. Dissociation is a process whereby the mind separates one or more aspects of its function (knowing, feeling, tasting, hearing, seeing, etc.) away from the normal stream of consciousness. Dissociation lies on a continuum ranging from the normal phenomena of day dreaming, fantasy, and "highway hypnosis" on the one end to the poly-fragmented (highly complex) multiple whose mind is split into hundreds (or thousands) of separate identities on the other end. This condition was formerly known as Multiple Personality Disorder (MPD), but was changed to Dissociative Identity Disorder (DID) in 1994 by the American Psychiatric Association with its publication of DSM-IV, in order to more accurately describe the disorder."

[2] Tom Hawkins passed away a few years ago and Diane Hawkins how leads Restoration in Christ Ministries.

[3] http://www.rcm-usa.org/ *Dissociative Identity Disorder: Recognizing and Restoring the Severely Abused*. Tom R. Hawkins, Ph.D.

CHAPTER TWO

INTRODUCTION TO THE BODY, SOUL, AND SPIRIT

Exploring Heavenly Places: a nice title, but how does the average Christian do such a thing? Many of us have been taught that to delve into the unseen is tantamount to engaging in occult philosophies. But it's not! New Age practitioners and faiths that embrace the supernatural do not point their followers to the true God, as manifested in the persons of Father, Son, and Holy Spirit. Rather, they consort with evil entities and seek after the very real experiences that are accessible in unrighteous spiritual realms. Yes, Satan is quite the imitator; but the original creation still belongs to God, and the right to explore it is the privilege of His children.

The words are so familiar:

> *In the beginning God created....And God said, Let us make man in our image, after our likeness: and let them have dominion over the fish of the sea, and over the fowl of the air, and over the cattle, and over all the earth, and over every creeping thing that creepeth upon the earth. So God created man in his own image, in the image of God created he him; male and female created he them. And God blessed them, and God said unto them, Be fruitful, and multiply, and replenish the earth, and subdue it: and have dominion over the fish of the sea, and over the fowl of the air, and over every living thing that moveth upon the earth...The LORD God formed man of the dust of the ground, and breathed into his nostrils the breath of life; and the man became a living soul.[1]*

We were created in His image, but what does that mean now that we live in a fallen world? Yes, dominion was handed over to Satan when Adam and Eve sinned, and God's plan for mankind was seemingly derailed; but the Savior was promised and:

> *When the fullness of the time had come, God sent forth His Son.[2]*

That Son, Jesus, exhibits *the brightness of His glory and the express image of His person,*[3] and we are to be conformed to His image.[4]

No other created being was made in His image. God is often referred to as the Trinity because of His three persons; but His makeup is also triune in that He possesses body, soul, and Spirit. His body is evident in Jesus' resurrected physical body, and there's no question of His spiritual nature. But does He have a soul? Yes!

> *[His] soul was grieved with the misery of Israel .*[5]

> *The righteous by faith shall live, and if he may draw back, My soul hath no pleasure in him.*[6]

How interesting it is that in His image mankind also possesses body, soul, and spirit.

God's original plan for mankind is again possible through His Son, Jesus, who declared:

> *Most assuredly, I say to you, he who believes in Me, the works that I do he will do also; and greater works than these he will do, because I go to My Father.*[7]

So it only makes sense that we not only have His permission but also are encouraged to look into the unseen. How else can we, like Jesus, do only what we see the Father doing? [8]

Clearly, as multi-dimensional beings, we have been designed to experience more than the time and space to which our bodies are confined.

> *By faith we understand that the worlds were framed by the word of God, so that the things which are seen were not made of things which are visible.*[9]

Therefore, we need to understand what the Bible has to say about our triune nature in order to comprehend the facets of interaction between the spiritual realms and ourselves.

[1] Genesis 1:1, 26-28; 2:7, KJV
[2] Galatians 4:4a
[3] Hebrews 1:3
[4] Romans 8:29
[5] Judges 10:16 KJV
[6] Hebrews 10:38 YLT
[7] John 14:12
[8] John 5:19
[9] Hebrews 11:3

CHAPTER THREE

UNDERSTANDING THE BODY: GOD'S ORIGINAL DESIGN

Who can resist the allure of a baby, especially during the first year of life? The frantic, helpless cry of a newborn; a little one gazing in awe at his hand, having just discovered that it is attached; giggles and laughs as a six-month-old chortles with joy when his tummy is tickled; dogged determination as the child discovers how to turn over, sit, crawl, stand, walk; funny little grins of amazement as hands plunge into a bowl of oatmeal, squishing all that wonderful gooey stuff through tiny fingers. And who can resist the endearing hugs and kisses; laughs and tears; waves and words, as he learns to show affection and communicate with more than tears? The baby is overwhelmingly occupied with his body—how it feels, and how he can make it do the things he sees others doing. He experiments and explores; he tries, fails, and tries again; and by his first birthday he has accomplished amazing feats of physical development. He is completely focused on the physical reality of life, and his bodily development now is key to future success in the transition from toddler, to child, to teen, to adult.

Throughout life we remain intimately aware of our bodies, knowing what they are capable of (or not!), knowing what makes them feel good as well as what hurts. Young adults may think or act like their bodies are invincible, but all too soon the aging process is realized. Wrinkles and gray hair appear; body parts start wearing out; and suddenly, or so it seems, movements and thought processes begin to slow down. How tempting it is to obsessively chase after the newest gimmick to maintain a youthful appearance or to be derailed by health issues and end up chasing an elusive cure-all. It may be hard to face, but we finally come to understand that death is an eventual certainty.

Bodies, undeniably stuck in the physical realm, are gifted with five senses that enable us to perceive time and space. Touch, taste, smell, hearing, and sight; so very familiar that we may take them for granted and assume, incorrectly, that they are as consigned to the physical reality as is flesh and bone. In His perfect design, God gave bodies the ability to interact dimensionally, even while confined to the world.

The importance of a body to God cannot be underestimated, whether the word is used in an individual sense or as a reference to the church as the Body of Christ.

> *And He is the head of the body, the church, who is the beginning, the firstborn from the dead, that in all things He may have the preeminence...now rejoice in my sufferings for you, and fill up in my flesh what is lacking in the afflictions of Christ, for the sake of His body, which is the church.[1]*

That God considers our bodies to be very special is evident in the beautiful words of Psalm 139, which tell how He lovingly handcrafted each of us.

> *For you formed my inward parts; you covered me in my mother's womb. I will praise you, for I am fearfully and wonderfully made; Marvelous are your works, And that my soul knows very well. My frame was not hidden from you, When I was made in secret, And skillfully wrought in the lowest parts of the earth. Your eyes saw my substance, being yet unformed. And in Your book they all were written, The days fashioned for me, When as yet there were none of them.[2]*

How often do we contemplate the enormity of those words? How often do we complain about the things we don't like about ourselves rather than praising God that we are His unique and perfectly designed masterpieces? Many years ago I (Barbara) wrote in the back of my Bible a quote from an unremembered source, "God made you exactly the way you are because He wants to spend eternity with someone exactly like you." I must admit I haven't always heeded those words; but like everyone else, have often fallen into the trap of wishing I could change myself into something better. However, the bottom line is that while our bodies are obviously essential—in fact, you might say we can't live without them—our lives are not to revolve around their physical needs. Jesus Himself said:

> *Take no thought for your life, what ye shall eat, or what ye shall drink; nor yet for your body, what ye shall put on. Is not the life more than meat, and the body than raiment? ...But seek ye first the kingdom of God, and his righteousness; and all these things shall be added unto you.*[3]

Ok, bodies are vital but we're not to obsess about them, so how are they to be viewed and used? What is their purpose? David must have understood that our bodies were created to be in relationship with God when he wrote:

> *O God, You are my God; Early will I seek You; My soul thirsts for You; My flesh longs for You In a dry and thirsty land where there is no water.*[4]

> *And, per Solomon's instruction, we are to trust in the LORD with all your heart, And lean not on your own understanding; In all your ways acknowledge Him, And He shall direct your paths. Do not be wise in your own eyes; Fear the LORD and depart from evil. It will be health to your flesh, And strength to your bones.*[5]

What conclusions can be drawn about our bodies as originally intended by God? A quick look back to the creation story in Genesis reveals:

- They are physical entities, formed of the dust of the earth and brought to life by God's own breath.
- We did not descend from other forms of life as various evolutionary theories would have us believe, but were created in God's image and given dominion over the entire earth.
- Male and female bodies were designed to come together and reproduce a multitude of children who would inhabit a perfect world.
- To be made in God's image implies that we were meant to look like Him—much like a sculpture, painting, or photograph portraying an original; or as a mirror image with a reflection that

is identical to the real.

- We were meant to commune with God; walking, talking, and even seeing Him, as did Adam and Eve; living bodily in a spiritual reality.

But wait; how can we know what God looks like? Does He have hands, feet, a nose, mouth, and ears? Some might argue that it's impossible to know; after all, how can we be certain? We can look to Jesus, the Man who is God.

[1] Colossians 1:18, 24
[2] Psalm 139:13-16
[3] Matthew 6:25, 33, KJV
[4] Psalm 63:1
[5] Proverbs 3:5-8

CHAPTER FOUR

UNDERSTANDING THE BODY: OUR PRESENT REALITY

In the beginning God created man in His image and said it was good, but Adam and Eve sinned and our bodies were cursed with death. As promised, Jesus, the perfectly sinless Son of God, came in bodily form; lived and died, taking our sins upon his body; was resurrected and spent forty days with His followers; ascended bodily into heaven; and lives eternally in His glorified and transformed body, thus becoming the first-fruit and making the redemption of our bodies possible. That takes care of the beginning and the end, but what about the in between where we now exist? God's word gives us a lot of direction. We may be temporarily confined to bodies and subject to the effects of sin—disease, destruction, death—but God still has a plan, and He has graciously let us in on it. It is of utmost importance that we internalize His truth:

> *Or do you not know that your body is the temple of the Holy Spirit who is in you, whom you have from God, and you are not your own? For you were bought at a price; therefore glorify God in your body and in your spirit, which are God's.*[1]

It's not uncommon for us to take great care of our important possessions such as homes, cars, toys, etc., because they are of value; expensive in terms of time, effort or money, we don't want them damaged. But how often we forget the cost Jesus paid to allow us to become the dwelling place of the Spirit of the Living God. The more we comprehend the enormity of what He's done for us, the more we want to honor Him in our bodies, and the more seriously we take scriptures such as:

> *He who guards his mouth preserves his life, But he who opens wide his lips shall have destruction.*[2]

> *Oh, clap your hand, all you peoples! Shout to God with the voice of triumph.*[3]

Whatever your hand finds to do, do it with your might.[4]

He who has ears to hear, let him hear [listen].[5]

Therefore do not let sin reign in your mortal body.[6]

If you confess with your mouth the Lord Jesus and believe in your heart that God has raised Him from the dead, you will be saved. For with the heart one believes unto righteousness, and with the mouth confession is made unto salvation.[7]

Flee sexual immorality. Every sin that a man does is outside the body, but he who commits sexual immorality sins against his own body.[8]

But I discipline my body and bring it into subjection.[9]

This will turn out for my deliverance...so now also Christ will be magnified in my body, whether by life or by death.[10]

What was that last phrase? *So now also Christ will be magnified in my body, whether by life or by death.* Sounds good, but what does that look like? Perhaps a few examples will help us understand more clearly.

Moses and the Israelites sang. Miriam and the women with her danced as they celebrated the deliverance of the Lord at the Red Sea. King David leapt and danced with joy in the streets of Jerusalem at the return of the ark from the Philistines.[11]

Consider Joseph; handsome, gifted, and much loved by his dad; but rejected by his ten older brothers out of jealousy. They dumped him into a cistern while they considered killing him, but sold him into slavery instead. Hauled off to Egypt, he served the captain of Pharaoh's guard, but his master's wife tried to seduce him. He refused her advances and ran away but was falsely accused and thrown into prison. Still, Joseph remained faithful to God, all the while earning the trust of the jailer and interpreting dreams for some of his prison mates. He asked one of them to mention his case to Pharaoh, but the man quickly forgot and Joseph remained locked away for two more years until Pharaoh had a dream and was desperate to know its meaning. When the former prisoner finally remembered, Joseph was brought to interpret the dream, gave an accurate word from the Lord, and was made second in command over all of Egypt. He knew what it meant to glorify God in his body, regardless of the physical suffering that was imposed upon it. Finally, reunited with his brothers, he forgave, comforted, and provided for them.[12] Joseph knew the truth; God is a restorer of those who seek Him.

Or, how about Daniel and his friends Shadrach, Meshach, and Abednego? Young men ripped from their homes and hauled off into slavery in Babylon, they were selected for special service to King Nebuchadnezzar. During their training, they were determined to honor God in their bodies and convinced the guard to serve only vegetables and water instead of the rich food and wine from the king's table. As a result, they surpassed all others in terms of wisdom and understanding and the king found them to be ten times better than all of the magicians and enchanters throughout his whole kingdom. As time went on, each man was challenged to abandon his faith in God and worship the king or suffer the consequences. The results of those threats are well known, for who hasn't heard of three men who survived a fiery furnace without even the smell of smoke on their bodies; or of Daniel's night in the lion's den where his body was unharmed, in great contrast to his accusers whose bodies were crushed before they even touched the floor.[13]

And don't forget Stephen, who cried out to God for the forgiveness of his murderers as he was stoned to death. Certainly his example must have impacted a young man named Saul who stood by and watched over the belongings of the killers; a young man we know today as the Apostle Paul.[14]

The list goes on as we examine the lives of biblical people who conducted themselves in such a way that attention was drawn to God; well documented examples of ordinary men in physical bodies who experienced the supernatural, undoubtedly with no clue of the impact that their stand for righteousness would have upon the world.

The way we use our bodies matters. We can honor God by making wise choices regarding what we watch, read, and listen to, as well as the activities in which we participate. We can bless others with the words of our mouth or destroy them with gossip; we can treat people with kindness or strike out with violence and cause injury. The choices we make every day as to the use of our bodies are not to be taken lightly:

> *...for we must all appear before the judgment seat of Christ, that each one may receive the things done in the body, according to what he has done, whether good or bad.*[15]

Remember the baby whose life revolves around his body? Such actions are necessary and appropriate for a time, but we cannot remain babes forever; we must grow up. Let us not be slow to learn:

> *For though by this time you ought to be teachers, you need someone to teach you again the first principles of the oracles of God; and you have come to need milk and not solid food. For everyone who partakes only of milk is unskilled in the word of righteousness, for he is a babe. But solid food belongs to those who are of full age, that is, those who by reason of use have their senses exercised to discern both good and evil.*[16]

Rather, let us follow the example set for us by Jesus:

> *...who, in the days of His flesh, when He had offered up prayers and supplications, with vehement cries and tears to Him who was able to save Him from death, and was heard because of His godly fear, though He was a Son, yet He learned obedience by the things which He suffered. And having been perfected, He became the author of eternal salvation to all who obey Him, called by God as High Priest according to the order of Melchizedek.*[17]

As we seek to follow His example, progressively becoming more and more conformed to His image, we will begin to do those things that He did, things that cannot be explained in the natural realm. And, as we learn to exercise discernment through the use of our physical senses, we will encounter the heavenly realms.

[1] Corinthians 6:19-20:
[2] Proverbs 13:3
[3] Psalm 47:1
[4] Ecclesiastes 9:10
[5] Matthew 13:9
[6] Romans 6:12
[7] Romans 10:9-10
[8] 1 Corinthians 6:18
[9] 1 Corinthians 9:27
[10] Philippians 1:19a, 20b
[11] Exodus 15; 2 Samuel 6:12-19
[12] Genesis 39-41
[13] Daniel 1, 3, 6
[14] Acts 7:54-60
[15] 2 Corinthians 5:10
[16] Hebrews 5:12-14
[17] Hebrews 5:7-10

CHAPTER FIVE

UNDERSTANDING THE BODY: THE MAN, JESUS

Jesus is identified both as the Creator and as a Man with a physical body:

> *In the beginning was the Word, and the Word was with God, and the Word was God. He was in the beginning with God. All things were made through Him, and without Him nothing was made that was made...And the Word became flesh and dwelt among us, and we beheld His glory, the glory as of the only begotten of the Father, full of grace and truth.*[1]

And this man, Jesus—the Creator; the Word; God—said:

> *If you had known Me, you would have known My Father also; and from now on you know Him and have seen Him...He who has seen Me has seen the Father*[2]

It follows that since it is His image in which we were created, we must resemble Him in our bodies.

God's original plan for people to dwell in communion with Him on the earth, enjoying His company as Adam and Eve did in the Garden of Eden, was thwarted when they chose to sin in their bodies by eating the forbidden fruit; wreaking havoc not only upon themselves but upon all succeeding generations. Death made an entrance and God declared:

> *Cursed is the ground for your sake; In toil you shall eat of it all the days of your life. Both thorns and thistles it shall bring forth for you, And you shall eat the herb of the field. In the sweat of your face you shall eat bread till you return to the ground, For out of it you were taken; For dust you are, And to dust you shall return.*[3]

Life in the body as we know it began not only with the curse of physical death, but also with a curse upon the very ground we walk

24

upon so that throughout all of our lives we struggle to survive. Biblical evidence of the impact of sin appeared swiftly as men used their bodies to dishonor God, committing acts of murder, rape, adultery, theft, lying, idolatry, and on and on. Indeed, only six chapters into the Bible we see that:

> *...the LORD saw that the wickedness of man was great in the earth, and that every intent of the thoughts of his heart was only evil continually. And the LORD was sorry that He had made man on the earth, and He was grieved in His heart.[4]*

As sin increased, various forms of infirmity soon began eating away at the bodies God had intended to live forever; leprosy, blindness, deafness, boils, infectious diseases, chronic wounds, itching, lameness; and again, the list goes on[5] None of us are exempt; all have suffered illness or injury; and all have sinned with our bodies. So what are we to do? Like Paul, we may cry:

> *O wretched man that I am! Who will deliver me from this body of death?[6]*

It's a valid question, and fortunately one that has a wonderful response, Jesus:

> *...who Himself bore our sins in His own body on the tree, that we, having died to sins, might live for righteousness—by whose stripes you were healed.[7]*

Time and again when we ask a question, Jesus is the answer. It was His body that was physically tortured and killed in a plot designed by evil to keep mankind enslaved forever; it was His body that carried our sins to the grave; it was His body that was resurrected, providing us with hope, healing, and a path to the redemption of our own bodies.

There are many questions and many belief systems regarding the body; in particular, the resurrection of the body of which much has been written, so let's keep it simple. Paul urged us to look to:

> *Jesus, the author and finisher of our faith[8] [as our example; for] now*

25

> *Christ is risen from the dead, and has become the firstfruits of those who have fallen asleep. For since by man came death, by Man also came the resurrection of the dead. For as in Adam all die, even so in Christ all shall be made alive.*[9]

It's important to note that Jesus was not the first to ever rise from the dead, having called others back to life before experiencing death personally; but He was the first man whose resurrected body would never die again. This is what makes Him our first-fruit, our example. Looking to Him, we see some interesting characteristics of His resurrected body.

- He was changed; transformed in a way that caused Him to be unrecognizable by those to whom He had not revealed Himself; as in His appearances to Mary Magdalene and the two on the road to Emmaus.[10]
- He was not limited by physical barriers, as evidenced when He suddenly appeared in the room with His followers. He could come and go at will, regardless of closed doors or walls.[11]
- His body was tangible, physical, as evidenced by eating food.[12]
- His body still bore the scars of His crucifixion, which implies that He didn't have a brand-new body but a perfectly restored and resurrected original.[13]
- He ascended in His body to heaven.[14]
- In His body, Jesus will return again.[15]

Even so, many questions remain. Will our resurrected bodies have the same characteristics? Will we be able to suddenly appear wherever we wish? If we have the same body, what will it look like? Will it be young or old? Will it carry scars? How can a body that has already turned back to dust be raised to become the same body it was at its demise? Until we experience our own resurrection, we will always have questions; so perhaps our best approach is simply to agree with the Apostle John:

> *Beloved, now we are children of God; and it has not yet been revealed*

what we shall be, but we know that when He is revealed, we shall be like Him, for we shall see Him as He is.[16]

We don't need to have all of the answers; just knowing that God has them allows us to continue on in faith:

...for our citizenship is in heaven, from which we also eagerly wait for the Savior, the Lord Jesus Christ, who will transform our lowly body that it may be conformed to His glorious body, according to the working by which He is able even to subdue all things to Himself.[17]

Perhaps a word of caution should be injected here. While the wonders of eternal life in a resurrected body are available to all, all will not receive them. It's unfortunate, but many will not heed the instruction not to:

...fear those who kill the body but cannot kill the soul. But rather fear Him who is able to destroy both soul and body in hell.[18]

A terrible fate, of which many are hesitant to speak, awaits those who choose to reject Christ Jesus.

Even before we reach our final destination of either eternal life with Christ or eternal damnation in hell, our bodies can be inhabited and/or influenced by spiritual beings, whether good or evil. Numerous biblical accounts tell of both angelic encounters and demonic oppression. How much better to choose righteousness and be filled with the presence of the Holy Spirit; how much better for our bodies to display evidence of Him as the believers did at Pentecost; how much better for our bodies to manifest the fruit of the Spirit as we operate in the gifts of the Spirit.

[1] John 1:1-3, 14
[2] John 14:7, 9b
[3] Genesis 3:17b-19
[4] Genesis 6:5-6
[5] Leviticus 19:14; 21:8; Deuteronomy 28:27; 1 Samuel 5:6; 2 Kings 5:27; Job 2:7; Mark 9:17-22
[6] Romans 7:24
[7] Peter 2:24
[8] Hebrews 12:2
[9] 1 Corinthians 15:20-22
[10] John 20:10-18
[11] Luke 24:36
[12] Luke 24:41-42
[13] Luke 24:37-40
[14] Acts 1:1-9
[15] Acts 1:10-11
[16] 1 John 3:2
[17] Philippians 3:20-21
[18] Matthew 10:28

CHAPTER SIX

THE SOUL OF MAN

Throughout the ages mankind has expressed himself through music, seeking to convey thoughts, feelings, and attitudes in a way that may be more memorable than the spoken word. Beginning in the late 1950s, a new musical genre emerged—soul—it's popularity exploding in the 60s. But the word 'soul', as with many other words in our language, has multiple synonyms, most of which are inadequate to express the hidden depths of the music. Combining elements of gospel and rhythm and blues, soul originally exemplified the Black experience in America but soon included not only Motown soul but also blue and brown-eyed soul; smooth and psychedelic soul; Detroit, Memphis, New Orleans, and British soul; Northern and Southern soul; and soul expressed as blues or jazz or even disco.[1]

As the music streamed across the transistor radios of the 60s with Sam and Dave crooning, "I'm a soul man..."[2] or The Music Explosion belting out the lyrics of *Little Bit O Soul*,[3] the church-going teen was also hearing and singing such tunes as, "Thank You, Lord, for saving my soul..."[4] "My soul in sad exile was out on life's sea..."[5] or, "He hideth my soul in the depths of His love and covers me there with His hand..."[6] To add to the mixed messages, those same teenagers entered high school and college and began studying such topics as philosophy, psychology, and world religion, only to discover that each one seemed to have a different take on the meaning of soul.

To the Christian, God's truth regarding a matter should be preeminent. In fact, we are promised that:

> *...you shall know the truth, and the truth shall set you free.*[7]

So what does the Bible says about the soul?

An in-depth word study using various commentaries would quickly reveal that the root words for soul (*nepes* in OT Hebrew, and psyche in NT Greek) occur more than 850 times in the Bible and, like soul music, are expressed in English using a variety of synonyms. These not only include 'soul' but also 'life', 'person', 'creature', 'appetite', 'mind', 'being', 'self'; and the list goes on. Additionally, each of the many Bible versions available may translate the same root word differently. Interesting, yes, but potentially overwhelming as well.

So, picture this: you are alone in a secluded place, perhaps even stranded on a mythical desert island, and you have nothing to read but a New King James version of the Bible. You're a brand-new believer but you've had no teaching at all about God's truths. Most likely, out of boredom, if nothing else, you'd eventually pick up the Bible and start to read; probably just like you would a novel, from beginning to end. So let's start in Genesis through Deuteronomy, commonly known as the Books of Moses; the Law; the Pentateuch; or to the Jews, the Torah; and search out some of the things the Holy Spirit might teach through God's written word as it is expressed in the New King James.

- *"See now, this city is near enough to flee to, and it is a little one; please let me escape there...and my soul shall live,"*[8] begged Lot when the angels told him to flee Sodom because God was about to destroy it. His use of soul indicates that it is alive and implies that dangerous circumstances threaten it with death.

- Isaac, instructed by Esau to make a *savory food, such as I love, and bring it to me that I may eat, that my soul may bless you before I die,*[9] makes it clear that one's soul can act volitionally to bless another person. The same phrase, 'soul may bless', is repeated three more times as the account continues.[10]

- Attraction and longing can be expressed by the soul as illustrated in the story of Shechem's feelings for Jacob's daughter Dinah.[11]

- Rachel died at the birth of her son Benjamin and her soul was described as departing.[12]

- After Joseph revealed himself to his brothers in Egypt, their past came back to haunt them and their souls were very troubled as they said to one another, *We are truly guilty concerning our brother, for we saw the anguish of his soul when he pleaded with us, and we would not hear; therefore this distress has come upon us.*[13]

- As Jacob spoke his last words to his sons he said, *"Simeon and Levi are brothers; Instruments of cruelty are in their dwelling place. Let not my soul enter their council."*[14] It is apparent that evil advice or association can influence the soul.

Leviticus, the book in which God's law is laid out for His people, includes ten references to soul indicating that it can be afflicted, atoned for, and can abhor individuals or things.[15]

Numbers confirms that souls may be sinned against, may become discouraged, may be afflicted, and may loathe things.[16]

A new concept is introduced in Deuteronomy that is repeated throughout the Bible; the soul not only can but also is encouraged to seek, love, and serve God in cooperation with the heart (or spirit), and to store up His words in the heart and soul. Additionally, life and abundance is promised for such obedience.

> *And the LORD your God will circumcise your heart and the heart of your descendants, to love the LORD your God with all your heart and with all your soul, that you may live...The LORD your God will make you abound in all the work of your hand, in the fruit of your body, in the increase of your livestock, and in the produce of your land for good. For the LORD will again rejoice over you for good as He rejoiced over your fathers, if you obey the voice of the LORD your God, to keep His commandments and His statutes which are written in this Book of the Law, and if you turn to the LORD your God with all your heart and with all your soul.*[17]

Conversely however, there are terrible consequences when the choice is made to be disobedient:

> *And among those nations you shall find no rest, nor shall the sole of your foot have a resting place; but there the LORD will give you a trembling heart, failing eyes, and anguish of soul.*[18]

Having now examined the Pentateuch, much has already been

discovered about the soul:

- The soul is associated with physical life, and death occurs when it departs.
- The soul experiences positive and negative emotions.
- Others can influence the soul.
- The soul can make choices to bless others, and to seek, love, and obey God—or not; it can sin.
- Atonement can be made for the soul.

In 1 Samuel, we are told that the soul of Jonathan was knit to the soul of David. So it appears that one person's soul can attach to another's, in this case out of a deep and abiding devotion in which Jonathan loved David as his own soul.[19]

Suffering plagued Job's life for a time when he lost everything except his life. Thus, the references to soul in the book of Job reflect a tremendous amount of anguish and include cursing of the soul as well as its consignment to, or redemption from, the Pit:

Why is light given to him who is in misery, and life to the bitter of soul.[20]

Can flavorless food be eaten without salt? Or is there any taste in the white of an egg? My soul refuses to touch them; they are as loathsome food to me.[21]

Therefore I will not restrain my mouth...I will complain in the bitterness of my soul.[22]

So that my soul chooses strangling And death rather than my body.[23]

My soul loathes life; I will give free course to my complaint, I will speak in the bitterness of my soul.[24]

How long will you torment my soul...?[25]

And now my soul is poured out because of my plight.[26]

Indeed I have not allowed my mouth to sin By asking for a curse on his soul.[27]

Yes, his soul draws near the Pit, And his life to the executioners.[28]

He will redeem his soul from going down to the Pit, and his life shall see the light.[29]

Over one hundred references to soul in Psalms and Proverbs reflect previous lessons learned and also introduce new truth. Even as we discover that there are terrible trials and places that the soul can experience, we are comforted by wonderful descriptions of how God rescues and ministers to us:

For You will not leave my soul in Sheol.[30]

The law of the LORD is perfect, converting the soul.[31]

He restores my soul.[32]

O LORD, You brought my soul up from the grave; You have kept me alive, that I should not go down to the pit.[33]

I will be glad and rejoice in Your mercy, For...You have known my soul in adversities.[34]

To deliver their soul from death, And to keep them alive in famine.[35]

But God will redeem my soul from the power of the grave.[36]

They have prepared a net for my steps; My soul is bowed down; They have dug a pit before me; Into the midst of it they themselves have fallen.[37]

[God] keeps our soul among the living, And does not allow our feet to be moved.[38]

For great is Your mercy toward me, And You have delivered my soul from the depths of Sheol.[39]

Unless the LORD had been my help, My soul would soon have settled in silence...In the multitude of anxieties within me, Your comforts delight my soul.[40]

My soul breaks with longing For Your judgments at all times.[41]

Then the swollen waters Would have gone over our soul...Our soul has escaped as a bird from the snare of the fowlers; The snare is broken, and we have escaped.[42]

Bring my soul out of prison That I may praise Your name; The righteous shall surround me, For You shall deal bountifully with me.[43]

He who keeps your soul, does He not know it?[44]

By humility and fear of the LORD *Are riches and honor and life. Thorns and snares are in the way of the perverse; He who guards his soul will be far from them.*[45]

Ecclesiastes teaches us that the things we do for ourselves, in our own strength, do not bring satisfaction to the soul:

If a man begets a hundred children and lives many years, so that the days of his years are many, but his soul is not satisfied with goodness...a stillborn child is better than he...All the labor of man is for his mouth, And yet the soul is not satisfied.[46]

With over thirty references to soul, the books of the prophets confirm the lessons already learned, and Isaiah contrasts the dire soul consequences of rejecting God with the wonders that He supplies to his children:

It shall even be as when a hungry man dreams, And look—he eats; But he awakes, and his soul is still empty; Or as when a thirsty man dreams, And look—he drinks; But he awakes, and indeed he is faint, And his soul still craves: So the multitude of all the nations shall be, Who fight against Mount Zion.[47]

The LORD *will guide you continually, And satisfy your soul in drought, And strengthen your bones; You shall be like a watered garden, And like a spring of water whose waters do not fail.*[48]

I will greatly rejoice in the LORD, *My soul shall be joyful in my God;*

For he has clothed me with the garments of salvation, He has covered me with the robe of righteousness, As a bridegroom decks himself with ornaments, And as a bride adorns herself with jewels.[49]

The New Testament is full of the story of redemption. Previous lessons still apply, but now we have the words of Jesus Himself as He gives warnings, instructions, and promises; often quoting from Old Testament scriptures:

And do not fear those who kill the body but cannot kill the soul. But, rather fear Him who is able to destroy both soul and body in hell.[50]

Take My yoke upon you and learn from Me, for I am gentle and lowly in heart, and you will find rest for your souls.[51]

And you shall love the Lord your God with all your heart, with all your soul, with all your mind, and with all your strength.[52]

In the early church the concept of souls being bound together is evident:

Now the multitude of those who believed were of one heart and soul; neither did anyone say that any of the things he possessed was his own, but they had all things in common.[53]

New Testament writers spoke of the power of God's word upon the soul and the salvation of the soul:

For the word of God is living and powerful, and sharper than any two-edged sword, piercing even to the division of soul and spirit, and of joints and marrow, and is a discerner of the thoughts and intents of the heart.[54]

Therefore lay aside all filthiness and overflow of wickedness, and receive with meekness the implanted word, which is able to save your souls.[55]

Though now you do not see Him, yet believing, you rejoice with joy inexpressible and full of glory, receiving the end of your faith—the salvation of your souls.[56]

Going back to the beginning in Genesis, one of the first lessons learned was that the soul has to do with the concept of life, of a living being. And fittingly, the Bible ends with the triumphant declaration of the living souls of Revelation 20:4:

> *And I saw thrones, and they sat on them, and judgment was committed to them. Then I saw the souls of those who had been beheaded for their witness to Jesus and for the word of God, who had not worshiped the beast or his image, and had not received his mark on their foreheads or on their hands. And they lived and reigned with Christ for a thousand years.*

What an indelible image of a soul committed to God; a soul that overcomes; a soul that has withstood the trials and temptations of life; a soul that is not confined to one of those horrible dark places such as the Pit, Sheol, or Death, but who lives in victory in the very Presence of God! The words of another old song come to mind, "It will be worth it all when we see Jesus; life's trials will seem so small when we see Christ..."[57]

[1] Wikipedia, the Free Encyclopedia; http://en.wikipedia.org/wiki/Soul_music

[2] *Soul Man*, by Isaac Hayes and David Porter, 1967; as recorded by Sam & Dave, Stax/Atlantic S-231

[3] *Little Bit O Soul*, by John Carter and Ken Lewis, 1964; as recorded by The Music Explosion, Laurie 3380—5/67

[4] *Thank You Lord For Saving My Soul*, S & B Sykes, 1940, 1945 New Spring (Admin. by Universal Music Publishing MGB Australia Pty)

[5] *My Soul in Sad Exile*, Henry L. Gilmour

[6] *He Hideth My Soul*, Francis J. Cosby

[7] John 8:32, NIV

[8] Genesis 19:20

[9] Genesis 27:4

[10] Genesis 27:19, 25, 31

[11] Genesis 34

[12] Genesis 35:18

[13] Genesis 42:21

[14] Genesis 49:5

[15] Leviticus 16:29, 31; 17:11; 23:27, 29, 32; 26:15, 30, 43

[16] Numbers 16:38; 21:4, 5; 29:7; 30:13

[17] Deuteronomy 30:6, 9-10

[18] Deuteronomy 28:65

[19] 1 Samuel 18

[20] Job 3:20

[21] Job 6:6-7

[22] Job 7:11

[23] Job 7:15

[24] Job 10:1

[25] Job 19:2

[26] Job 30:16

[27] Job 31:30

[28] Job 33:22

[29] Job 33:30

[30] Psalm 16:10

[31] Psalm 19:7

[32] Psalm 23:3

[33] Psalm 30:3
[34] Psalm 31:7
[35] Psalm 33:19
[36] Psalm 49:15
[37] Psalm 57:6
[38] Psalm 66:9
[39] Psalm 86:13
[40] Psalm 94:17, 19
[41] Psalm 119:20
[42] Psalm 124:5, 7
[43] Psalm 142:7
[44] Proverbs 24:12
[45] Proverbs 22:4-5
[46] Ecclesiastes 6:3, 7
[47] Isaiah 29:8
[48] Isaiah 58:11
[49] Isaiah 61:10
[50] Matthew 10:28
[51] Matthew 11:29
[52] Mark 12:30
[53] Acts 4:32
[54] Hebrews 4:12
[55] James 1:21
[56] 1 Peter 1:8-9
[57] *It Will Be Worth It All*, Esther Kerr Rushthoi

CHAPTER SEVEN
THE SPIRIT OF MAN

In the days of rabbit ears and black and white television, viewing choices were limited. But one cold, rainy day I (Barbara) was fortunate enough to catch the tale of George and Marion Kerby, two fun-loving ghosts trying to do a good deed that would get them out of limbo and into heaven. The movie was *Topper*, and the fact that it was already about thirty years old didn't dampen my enthusiasm for the story. Perhaps it was just because I was bored that I enjoyed it so much; or perhaps I fell prey to the mystique that surrounds the concept of spirits who once inhabited human bodies, in which case I was not alone. *Topper*, released in 1938, spawned two sequels in 1938 and 1941, a television series in 1953, and a television pilot in 1973; and *Topper* is not alone in its ability to enchant viewers with ideas about what happens after we die. In *Carousel*, Billy Bigelow was turned away from heaven's gate until his spirit returned to earth and alleviated all of the distress he'd caused in his lifetime. In *Here Comes Mr. Jordan*, remade in 1978 as *Heaven Can Wait*, the spirit of a sports figure accidentally killed before his time is sent back to earth to inhabit the body of someone whose time is up.[1] And the list goes on, for who can forget later films and TV series such as *Ghost*, *The Sixth Sense*, or *Medium*? But, as entertaining as these media presentations may be, do they give us an accurate picture of the spirit of man? Unfortunately, many people seem to integrate such popular stories into their own personal beliefs, perhaps because they feel so good and offer such happy explanations to perplexing questions. However, the Christian must turn to the only truth that is valid for information regarding the spirit of man—the word of God.

As we have seen, the Bible is clear that man is multidimensional—a triune being consisting of three parts:

> *Now may the God of peace Himself sanctify you completely; and may your whole spirit, soul, and body be preserved blameless at the coming of our Lord Jesus Christ.*[2]

Several other things are also clear: God is the creator of man's spirit;

without the spirit, there is no physical life; and outside of Christ, our spirits are dead, or separated from God

> *Thus says the LORD, who stretches out the heavens, lays the foundation of the earth, and forms the spirit of man within him.[3]*

> *No one has power over the spirit to retain the spirit, And no one has power in the day of death.[4]*

> *...for as the body without the spirit is dead, so faith without works is dead also.[5]*

> *And you He made alive, who were dead in trespasses and sins, in which you once walked according to the course of this world, according to the prince of the power of the air, the spirit who now works in the sons of disobedience.[6]*

We understand the body because we can see and touch it; and we have a fair comprehension of the soul because it is generally understood to have to do with our mind, will, and emotion. But, what of the spirit? It is so much more esoteric, and every '–ism' that exists seems to offer a different slant on it. Perhaps some of the confusion is because the triune being of man exists in a multidimensional universe of which he has little or no comprehension. Many may assume that if something is outside of the realms of time and space it doesn't really exist but is simply make-believe or science fiction. Where such ignorance exists, the enemy steps in and creates confusion in the form of superstition and false belief systems. Certainly, down through the ages, civilization after civilization has fallen into paganism; worshiping unseen spirits of the moon, the harvest, the sun, whatever seemed important to them; creating their own spiritual deities because they did not comprehend the truth. Unfortunately, evil not only exists in spirit form but also works overtime to skew mankind's understanding of the spiritual realm. Man can even be inhabited or possessed by evil spirits:

- A spirit of jealousy came upon a man[7]
- A distressing spirit overcame Saul.[8]
- There are also perverse spirits, false spirits, lying spirits, foul

spirits, de ant spirits, and all manner of evil and unclean spirits that bring destruction upon mankind.[9]

That's the bad news; and the enemy would love for us to believe that's all there is. BUT (and it's a big but), while there are many kinds of spirits, only mankind shares the image of God; so it is reasonable to assume that our spirit is meant to be a mirror image of His, and His word shows us the truth. The spirit of man is the designation of that aspect of existence that is non-corporeal and immaterial. Its Latin derivation (as with the Hebrew and Greek words in the Bible, *ruach* and *pneuma*) denotes blowing or breathing (Job 41:16; Isaiah 25:4). So the noun, *spiritus* signifies breath and life. God, the source of all life, is himself Spirit (John 4:24). He put a spirit within all human beings so that they could commune with him in his realm and in his nature. A Christian's experience of Jesus Christ is made real when that person experiences the Spirit of Jesus Christ in his or her spirit.[10]

Good news indeed! The evidence is clear in scripture that we receive revelation from God through His Spirit—things that man alone could not otherwise comprehend.

> *But God has revealed them to us through His Spirit. For the Spirit searches all things, yes, the deep things of God. For what man knows the things of a man except the spirit of the man which is in him? Even so no one knows the things of God except the Spirit of God. Now we have received, not the spirit of the world, but the Spirit who is from God, that we might know the things that have been freely given to us by God. These things we also speak, not in words which man's wisdom teaches but which the Holy Spirit teaches, comparing spiritual things with spiritual. But the natural man does not receive the things of the Spirit of God, for they are foolishness to him; nor can he know them, because they are spiritually discerned.[11]*

> *But there is a spirit in man, And the breath of the Almighty gives him understanding.[12]*

The Lord motivates us through our spirits to accomplish His work:

So the LORD stirred up the spirit of Zerubbabel the son of Shealtiel, governor of Judah, and the spirit of Joshua the son of Jehozadak, the high priest, and the spirit of all the remnant of the people; and they came and worked on the house of the LORD of hosts, their God.[13]

For as many as are led by the Spirit, these are the sons of God.[14]

And a man of understanding is of calm spirit. [15]

The spirit of a man will sustain him in sickness, But who can bear a broken spirit?[16]

The spirit of a man is the lamp of the LORD, Searching all the inner depths of his heart.[17]

The child grew and became strong in spirit.[18]

God's power over evil spirits is evident as both Jesus and His followers cast out evil spirits:

When evening had come, they brought to Him many who were demon-possessed. And He cast out the spirits with a word, and healed all who were sick.[19]

The fruit of God's Spirit is available within in our spirits:

But the fruit of the Spirit is love, joy, peace, longsuffering, kindness, goodness, faithfulness, gentleness, self-control. Against such there is no law.[20]

God is so gracious to provide all the instruction and good examples necessary to deal with anything, including spiritual matters, if we only seek His truth:

A man's pride will bring him low, But the humble in spirit will retain honor.[21]

I will pray with the spirit, and I will also pray with the understanding. I will sing with the spirit.[22]

Brethren, if a man is overtaken in any trespass, you who are spiritual restore such a one in a spirit of gentleness, considering yourself lest you also be tempted.[23]

Joseph was so sold out to God that even the pagan king acknowledged it:

And Pharaoh said to his servants, 'Can we find such a one as this, a man in whom is the Spirit of God?'[24]

Daniel was introduced to Belshazzar as:

...a man in your kingdom in whom is the Spirit of the Holy God...light and understanding and wisdom, like the wisdom of the gods, were found in him.[25]

The life of Barnabas portrays how evangelism grows out of the fullness of the Spirit of God:

...for he was a good man, full of the Holy Spirit and of faith. And a great many people were added to the Lord.[26]

We are to be discerning of spiritual things:

Beloved, do not believe every spirit, but test the spirits, whether they are of God; because many false prophets have gone out into the world.[27]

Yes, we are to test the spirits; so here we are, right back at the movies. What about all of that? Is it OK to talk to the dead? Do our spirits have opportunities to come back and make things right after we die? Again, the Bible is specific. King Saul, so desperate for a prophetic word that he made a very bad decision that cost him greatly. The entire account is related here because it is so very relevant for today:

Now Samuel had died, and all Israel had lamented for him and buried him in Ramah, in his own city. And Saul had put the mediums and the spiritists out of the land. Then the Philistines gathered together, and came and encamped at Shunem. So Saul gathered all Israel together, and they encamped at Gilboa. When Saul saw the army of the Philistines, he was afraid, and his heart trembled greatly. And when Saul inquired of the LORD, the LORD did not answer him, either by dreams or by Urim or by the prophets. Then Saul said to his servants, "Find me a woman who is a medium, that

I may go to her and inquire of her." And his servants said to him, "In fact, there is a woman who is a medium at En Dor." So Saul disguised himself and put on other clothes, and he went, and two men with him; and they came to the woman by night. And he said, "Please conduct a séance for me, and bring up for me the one I shall name to you." Then the woman said to him, "Look, you know what Saul has done, how he has cut off the mediums and the spiritists from the land. Why then do you lay a snare for my life, to cause me to die?" And Saul swore to her by the LORD, saying, "As the LORD lives, no punishment shall come upon you for this thing." Then the woman said, "Whom shall I bring up for you?" And he said, "Bring up Samuel for me." When the woman saw Samuel, she cried out with a loud voice. And the woman spoke to Saul, saying, "Why have you deceived me? For you are Saul!" And the king said to her, "Do not be afraid. What did you see?" And the woman said to Saul, "I saw a spirit ascending out of the earth." So he said to her, "What is his form?" And she said, "An old man is coming up, and he is covered with a mantle." And Saul perceived that it was Samuel, and he stooped with his face to the ground and bowed down. Now Samuel said to Saul, "Why have you disturbed me by bringing me up?" And Saul answered, "I am deeply distressed; for the Philistines make war against me, and God has departed from me and does not answer me anymore, neither by prophets nor by dreams. Therefore I have called you, that you may reveal to me what I should do." Then Samuel said: "So why do you ask me, seeing the LORD has departed from you and has become your enemy? And the LORD has done for Himself as He spoke by me. For the LORD has torn the kingdom out of your hand and given it to your neighbor, David. Because you did not obey the voice of the LORD nor execute His fierce wrath upon Amalek, therefore the LORD has done this thing to you this day. Moreover the LORD will also deliver Israel with you into the hand of the Philistines. And tomorrow you and your sons will be with me. The LORD will also deliver the army of Israel into the hand of the Philistines." Immediately Saul fell full length on the ground, and was dreadfully afraid because of the words of Samuel. And there was no strength in him, for he had eaten no food all day or all night.[28]

God's opinion of man seeking after the spirits of the dead is quite clear:

> *A man or a woman who is a medium, or who has familiar spirits, shall surely be put to death; they shall stone them with stones. Their blood shall be upon them.*[29]

And He doesn't grant second chances after death either, for:

> *...it is appointed for men to die once, but after this the judgment.* [30]

But once again, we have really good news:

> *Christ was offered once to bear the sins of many. To those who eagerly wait for Him He will appear a second time, apart from sin, for salvation.*[31]

Jesus is again the answer to our every question—whether in regard to the things of this world, or the things of the spiritual realm of which we have so little comprehension. And it gets even better for we have God's amazing promise:

> *And you, being dead in your trespasses and the uncircumcision of your flesh, He has made alive together with Him, having forgiven you all trespasses, having wiped out the handwriting of requirements that was against us, which was contrary to us. And He has taken it out of the way, having nailed it to the cross. Having disarmed principalities and powers, He made a public spectacle of them, triumphing over them in it.*[32]

[1] Wikipedia; http://en.wikipedia.org/wiki/Topper_%28 lm%29; http://en.wikipedia.org/wiki/Carousel_%28 lm%29; http://en.wikipedia.org/wiki/Here_Comes_Mr._Jordan

[2] 1 Thessalonians 5:23

[3] Zechariah 12:1

[4] Ecclesiastes 8:8

[5] James 2:26

[6] Ephesians 2:1-2

[7] Numbers 5:30

[8] 1 Samuel 16:16

[9] Isaiah 19:14; Micah 2:11; Matthew 12:43-46; 1 Kings 22:22-23; Luke 11:24; 1 Thessalonians 4:8

[10] Elwell, W. A., & Comfort, P. W. (2001). *Tyndale Bible dictionary*. Tyndale reference library. Wheaton, Ill.: Tyndale House Publishers.

[11] 1 Corinthians 2:10-14

[12] Job 32:8

[13] Haggai 1:14-15

[14] Romans 8:14

[15] Proverbs 17:27b

[16] Proverbs 18:14

[17] Proverbs 20:27

[18] Luke 1:80

[19] Matthew 8:16

[20] Galatians 5:22-23

[21] Proverbs 29:23

[22] 1 Corinthians 14:15

[23] Galatians 6:1

[24] Genesis 41:38

[25] Daniel 5:11

[26] Acts 11:24

[27] 1 John 4:1

[28] 1 Samuel 28:3-20

[29] Leviticus 20:27

[30] Hebrews 9:27

[31] Hebrews 9:28

[32] Colossians 2:13-15

CHAPTER EIGHT
MATTERS OF THE HEART

Have you ever played a game of word association in which each person must indicate the very first word that comes to mind when another word is spoken? The end result can be hilarious as the original word morphs into something completely different and totally unexpected; and the more players, the stranger it gets. Word association might also be a tool that a psychologist would use in an attempt to learn more about a patient's underlying issues; or by a market researcher in an effort to ensure the proper message is conveyed in the promotion of a product.

What is the first thing that comes to your mind at the mention of the word 'heart'? If you've just been dumped by the love of your life, it might be broken. Around February 14, you may respond with valentines or flowers, something to do with an expression of love. But if you are a cardiac patient, it's more likely that you will think of such words as angina, pacemaker, bypass, hospital, medicine, fear, or death. It all depends on the individual point of reference. In written or verbal communication, context generally defines the meaning of heart. We easily differentiate between the physical organ beating away in our chests and a heart-shaped image on a valentine; a reference to the center of something, as in artichoke hearts; or a representation of one's feelings or emotions. So it should come as no surprise that, as in everyday communication, the Bible also refers to heart in a variety of ways that validate our personal experience.**On the sixth day of creation:**

> *God said, "Let Us make man in Our image, according to Our likeness; let them have dominion over the fish of the sea, over the birds of the air, and over the cattle, over all the earth and over every creeping thing that creeps on the earth." So God created man in His own image; in the image of God He created him; male and female He created them...Then God saw everything that He had made, and indeed it was very good.*[1]

What were those last few words again? *Indeed, it was very good.* So what a sad commentary it is that within just ten generations:

> ...*the* LORD *saw that the wickedness of man was great in the earth, and that every intent of the thoughts of his heart was only evil continually. And the* LORD *was sorry that He had made man on the earth, and He was grieved in His heart.*[2]

God's original intent was that man's heart would mirror His own, but it was quickly corrupted once Adam and Eve made the choice to be disobedient, and it appears that the heart became the battleground of good versus evil. On the one hand, Jesus died for us so that:

> *Christ may dwell in your hearts through faith.*[3]

Yet, on the other hand:

> ...*the devil comes and takes away the word out of their hearts, lest they should believe and be saved.*[4]

Scriptures shed light on affairs of the heart, with God always making a way for mankind to be reconciled to Himself, and evil always scheming to mess things up:

> *And I will make an everlasting covenant with them, that I will not turn away from doing them good; but I will put My fear in their hearts so that they will not depart from Me.*[5]

> *But Peter said, "Ananias, why has Satan filled your heart to lie to the Holy Spirit and keep back part of the price of the land for yourself?"*[6]

> *Now a certain woman named Lydia heard us. She was a seller of purple from the city of Thyatira, who worshiped God. The Lord opened her heart to heed the things spoken by Paul.*[7]

> *For those who are such do not serve our Lord Jesus Christ, but their own belly, and by smooth words and flattering speech deceive the hearts of the simple.*[8]

> *For God has put it into their hearts to fulfill His purpose, to be of one mind, and to give their kingdom to the beast, until the words of*

God are fulfilled.[9]

A good man out of the good treasure of his heart brings forth good; and an evil man out of the evil treasure of his heart brings forth evil. For out of the abundance of the heart his mouth speaks.[10]

But what is the context of the word heart that the Bible uses so frequently, over 900 times in fact? Mr. Spock or other very logical left-brain thinkers might have a tremendous amount of difficulty with the term. To them, 'heart' means the physical organ beating in our chests, and the concept of an immaterial heart is illogical and makes no sense. But surely God doesn't mean for His word to be confusing, so let's examine it for some clues as to the definition and function of the heart.

We have already determined that man is a triune being—body, soul, and spirit—so where does the heart reside? The physical aspect as a part of the body is obvious, the intangible or spiritual less so. Does it reside in the soul, the spirit, or both? Scriptures do not clearly state the answer, but there is evidence to suggest the heart is present in each aspect of a person:

- The heart does not appear to be exclusively a part of the soul. Repeatedly, scriptures list the two separately as we are encouraged to seek or serve the Lord with heart **and** soul,[11] which could imply that the heart must exist in the spirit.

- The Bible uses the words 'spirit' and 'heart' frequently in such a way as to imply that the heart is closely associated with the spirit.

- While the implication could be that the heart resides within the spirit, a case could also be made that it resides in the soul as well. If the word 'heart' in any of the scriptures below could refer to the soul, then the verses might be referring to both soul and spirit.

Then everyone came whose heart was stirred, and everyone whose spirit was willing.[12]

But Sihon king of Heshbon would not let us pass through, for the

LORD your God hardened his spirit and made his heart obstinate, that He might deliver him into your hand, as it is this day.[13]

...that their heart melted; and there was no spirit in them any longer because of the children of Israel.[14]

Create in me a clean heart, O God, and renew a steadfast spirit within me.[15]

The sacrifices of God are a broken spirit, A broken and a contrite heart—These, O God, You will not despise.[16]

I call to remembrance my song in the night; I meditate within my heart, And my spirit makes diligent search.[17]

Therefore my spirit is overwhelmed within me; My heart within me is distressed.[18]

A merry heart makes a cheerful countenance, But by sorrow of the heart the spirit is broken.[19]

For thus says the High and Lofty One Who inhabits eternity, whose name is Holy: "I dwell in the high and holy place, With him who has a contrite and humble spirit, To revive the spirit of the humble, And to revive the heart of the contrite ones."[20]

Cast away from you all the transgressions which you have committed, and get yourselves a new heart and a new spirit. For why should you die, O house of Israel?[21]

I will give you a new heart and put a new spirit within you; I will take the heart of stone out of your flesh and give you a heart of flesh.[22]

But when his heart was lifted up, and his spirit was hardened in pride, he was deposed from his kingly throne, and they took his glory from him.[23]

...rather let it be the hidden person of the heart, with the incorruptible beauty of a gentle and quiet spirit, which is very precious in the sight of God.[24]

It appears very possible that the heart does exist in each part of our being—body, soul, and spirit. But regardless of where it resides, one thing is abundantly clear; the heart, in its fallen state, *is deceitful above all things, And desperately wicked.*[25]

[1] Genesis 1:26-27, 31

[2] Genesis 6:5-6

[3] Ephesians 3:17

[4] Luke 8:12

[5] Jeremiah 32:40

[6] Acts 5:3

[7] Acts 16:14

[8] Romans 16:18

[9] Revelation 17:17

[10] Luke 6:45

[11] Deuteronomy 4:29, 11:13; Joshua 22:5; 1 Kings 2:4; 2 Kings 23:25; 1 Chronicles 22:19; 2 Chronicles 15:15; Matthew 22:37; Luke 10:27

[12] Exodus 35:21

[13] Deuteronomy 2:30

[14] Joshua 5:1

[15] Psalm 51:10

[16] Psalm 51:17

[17] Psalm 77:6

[18] Psalm 143:4

[19] Proverbs 15:13

[20] Isaiah 57:15

[21] Ezekiel 18:31

[22] Ezekiel 36:26

[23] Daniel 5:20

[24] 1 Peter 3:4

[25] Jeremiah 17:9

CHAPTER NINE

CONDITIONS OF THE HEART

We often fictionalize and laugh at the concept of an evil heart, enjoying tales of black-hearted pirates and evil black knights, or joking about someone with a cold or hard heart. One of our songs when I (Barbara) sang barbershop with the Sweet Adelines was *Hard Hearted Hannah*. She was described as the vamp from Savannah, the meanest girl in town; and she had quite a reputation for loving and leaving all the men unlucky enough to encounter her. It was fun to sing and funny to observe with our added choreography, but unfortunately it's really not a laughing matter. There is nothing so serious in life as a hard heart, such as with Pharaoh who repeatedly hardened his heart when there was relief from the plagues, until finally God made it a permanent condition.[1] The consequences are dire:

> *For it was of the LORD to harden their hearts, that they should come against Israel in battle, that He might utterly destroy them, and that they might receive no mercy, but that He might destroy them, as the LORD had commanded Moses.[2]*

> *So it was, in the morning, when the wine had gone from Nabal, and his wife had told him these things, that his heart died within him, and he became like a stone. Then it happened, after about ten days, that the LORD struck Nabal, and he died.[3]*

> *But when his heart was lifted up, and his spirit was hardened in pride, he was deposed from his kingly throne, and they took his glory from him.[4]*

> *Today, if you will hear His voice: "Do not harden your hearts, as in the rebellion, As in the day of trial in the wilderness, When your fathers tested Me; They tried Me, though they saw My work. For forty years I was grieved with that generation, And said, 'It is a people who go astray in their hearts, And they do not know My ways.' So I swore in My wrath, 'They shall not enter My rest.'"[5]*

But he who hardens his heart will fall into calamity.[6]

Yes, they made their hearts like flint, refusing to hear the law and the words which the LORD of hosts had sent by His Spirit through the former prophets. Thus great wrath came from the LORD of hosts.[7]

And when He had looked around at them with anger, being grieved by the hardness of their hearts...[8]

For they had not understood about the loaves, because their heart was hardened.[9]

Later He appeared to the eleven as they sat at the table; and He rebuked their unbelief and hardness of heart, because they did not believe those who had seen Him after He had risen.[10]

But in accordance with your hardness and your impenitent heart you are treasuring up for yourself wrath in the day of wrath and revelation of the righteous judgment of God.[11]

Consider and contrast the softened, flexible and receptive heart, as God desires it to be:

Because your heart was tender, and you humbled yourself before the LORD when you heard what I spoke against this place and against its inhabitants...I also have heard you, says the LORD.[12]

Keep my commands and live, And my law as the apple of your eye. Bind them on your fingers; Write them on the tablet of your heart.[13]

The wise in heart will receive commands.[14]

A sound heart is life to the body.[15]

The king's heart is in the hand of the LORD, Like the rivers of water; He turns it wherever He wishes.[16]

As in water face reflects face, So a man's heart reveals the man.[17]

He who keeps his command will experience nothing harmful; And a wise man's heart discerns both time and judgment.[18]

Therefore my heart shall resound like a harp for Moab.[19]

Then you shall see and become radiant, And your heart shall swell with joy.[20]

Then I will give them one heart, and I will put a new spirit within them, and take the stony heart out of their flesh, and give them a heart of flesh.[21]

Then I will give them a heart to know Me, that I am the LORD; and they shall be My people, and I will be their God, for they shall return to Me with their whole heart.[22]

But this is the covenant that I will make with the house of Israel after those days, says the LORD: I will put My law in their minds, and write it on their hearts; and I will be their God, and they shall be My people.[23]

He who believes in Me, as the Scripture has said, out of his heart will flow rivers of living water.[24]

Nevertheless He did not leave Himself without witness, in that He did good, gave us rain from heaven and fruitful seasons, filling our hearts with food and gladness.[25]

When we speak of 'getting to the heart of a matter' it is generally understood that we want to discover a central issue, and it seems that the heart is indeed the central issue of our lives. It is here that our true motivations and intentions are hidden, unseen by anyone except God Himself. It is here where our actions are initiated. It is here that we store our treasures, as if hidden in a bank vault. It is here we experience both condemnation and redemption:

Then everyone came whose heart was stirred, and everyone whose spirit was willing, and they brought the LORD's offering for the work of the tabernacle of meeting, for all its service, and for the holy garments. They came, both men and women, as many as had a willing heart, and brought earrings and nose rings, rings and necklaces, all jewelry of gold, that is, every man who made an offering of gold to the LORD.[26]

But the LORD said to Samuel, "Do not look at his appearance or at his physical stature, because I have refused him. For the LORD *does not see as man sees; for man looks at the outward appearance, but the* LORD *looks at the heart."*[27]

And David's heart condemned him after he had numbered the people. So David said to the LORD, *"I have sinned greatly in what I have done; but now, I pray, O* LORD, *take away the iniquity of Your servant, for I have done very foolishly."*[28]

They devise iniquities: "We have perfected a shrewd scheme." Both the inward thought and the heart of man are deep.[29]

For the foolish person will speak foolishness, And his heart will work iniquity: To practice ungodliness, To utter error against the LORD, *To keep the hungry unsatisfied, And he will cause the drink of the thirsty to fail.*[30]

Brood of vipers! How can you, being evil, speak good things? For out of the abundance of the heart the mouth speaks. A good man out of the good treasure of his heart brings forth good things, and an evil man out of the evil treasure brings forth evil things.[31]

But those things which proceed out of the mouth come from the heart, and they defile a man. For out of the heart proceed evil thoughts, murders, adulteries, fornications, thefts, false witness, blasphemies.[32]

But immediately, when Jesus perceived in His spirit that they reasoned thus within themselves, He said to them, "Why do you reason about these things in your hearts?"[33]

He answered and said to them, "Well did Isaiah prophesy of you hypocrites, as it is written: 'These people honor Me with their lips, but their heart is far from Me.'"[34]

Now as the people were in expectation, and all reasoned in their hearts about John, whether he was the Christ or not.[35]

For where your treasure is, there your heart will be also.[36]

And because you are sons, God has sent forth the Spirit of His Son into your hearts, crying out, "Abba, Father!"[37]

Therefore judge nothing before the time, until the Lord comes, who will both bring to light the hidden things of darkness and reveal the counsels of the hearts. Then each one's praise will come from God.[38]

...rather let it be the hidden person of the heart, with the incorruptible beauty of a gentle and quiet spirit, which is very precious in the sight of God.[39]

And by this we know that we are of the truth, and shall assure our hearts before Him. For if our heart condemns us, God is greater than our heart, and knows all things. Beloved, if our heart does not condemn us, we have confidence toward God.[40]

Throughout the scriptures we find verses contrasting the righteous heart and the evil heart. It makes sense that man would choose to have his heart described as loyal, upright, willing, faithful, glad, perfect, or merry rather than boastful, proud, wicked, deceitful, arrogant, perverse, or haughty; but apparently that's not the case. Instead of heeding the oft repeated admonition to:

...love the Lord your God with all your heart, with all your soul, with all your mind, and with all your strength.[41]

So many people today:

...like sheep have gone astray; We have turned, every one, to his own way.[42]

How sad that is, for without the redemption of the heart, the individual must live in a state of brokenness, with the spiritual defects carrying over and affecting day-to-day life in the physical realm:

I am feeble and severely broken; I groan because of the turmoil of my heart.[43]

Reproach has broken my heart, And I am full of heaviness; I looked for someone to take pity, but there was none; And for comforters, but I found none.[44]

A merry heart makes a cheerful countenance, But by sorrow of the heart the spirit is broken.[45]

A merry heart does good, like medicine, But a broken spirit dries the bones.[46]

My heart within me is broken because of the prophets; All my bones shake. I am like a drunken man, And like a man whom wine has overcome, Because of the LORD, And because of His holy words.[47]

Sigh therefore, son of man, with a breaking heart, and sigh with bitterness before their eyes.[48]

Their heart is divided; Now they are held guilty. He will break down their altars; He will ruin their sacred pillars.[49]

We would do well to heed God's word in regard to the heart; and whether in the context of the Old or New Testaments, the message remains the same:

I make this covenant and this oath, not with you alone, but with him who stands here with us today before the LORD our God, as well as with him who is not here with us today...so that there may not be among you man or woman or family or tribe, whose heart turns away today from the LORD our God, to go and serve the gods of these nations, and that there may not be among you a root bearing bitterness or wormwood; and so it may not happen, when he hears the words of this curse, that he blesses himself in his heart, saying, "I shall have peace, even though I follow the dictates of my heart"—as though the drunkard could be included with the sober. The LORD would not spare him; for then the anger of the LORD and His jealousy would burn against that man, and every curse that is written in this book would settle on him, and the LORD would blot out his name from under heaven.[50]

The word is near you, in your mouth and in your heart (that is, the word of faith which we preach): that if you confess with your mouth the Lord Jesus and believe in your heart that God has raised Him from the dead, you will be saved. For with the heart one believes unto righteousness, and with the mouth confession is made unto salvation.[51]

It doesn't get much clearer than that!

[1] Exodus 7-14
[2] Joshua 11:20
[3] 1 Samuel 25:37-38
[4] Daniel 5:20
[5] Psalm 95:7b-11
[6] Proverbs 28:14
[7] Zechariah 7:12
[8] Mark 3:5
[9] Mark 6:52
[10] Mark 16:14
[11] Romans 2:5
[12] 2 Kings 22:19
[13] Proverbs 7:2-3
[14] Proverbs 10:8
[15] Proverbs 14:30
[16] Proverbs 21:1
[17] Proverbs 27:19
[18] Ecclesiastes 8:5
[19] Isaiah 16:11
[20] Isaiah 60:5a
[21] Ezekiel 11:19
[22] Jeremiah 24:7
[23] Jeremiah 31:33
[24] John 7:38
[25] Acts 14:17
[26] Exodus 35:21-22
[27] 1 Samuel 16:7
[28] 2 Samuel 24:10
[29] Psalm 64:6
[30] Isaiah 32:6
[31] Matthew 12:34-35
[32] Matthew 15:18-19
[33] Mark 2:8
[34] Mark 7:6
[35] Luke 3:15

[36] Luke 12:34
[37] Galatians 4:6
[38] 1 Corinthians 4:5
[39] 1 Peter 3:4
[40] 1 John 3:19-21
[41] Mark 12:30
[42] Isaiah 53:6
[43] Psalm 38:8
[44] Psalm 69:20
[45] Proverbs 15:13
[46] Proverbs 17:22
[47] Jeremiah 23:9
[48] Ezekiel 21:6
[49] Hosea 10:2
[50] Deuteronomy 29:14-15, 18-20
[51] Romans 10:8-10

CHAPTER TEN

THE WILL

With apologies to linguists who love the study of grammar, I (Barbara) must confess that I hated the seemingly endless hours of diagramming sentences and studying the differences between nouns, verbs, adjectives, adverbs, conjunctions, articles, phrases, sentences, paragraphs, periods, commas, exclamation and question marks, asterisks, parentheses, colons, semi-colons... Even that last sentence seemed like it would never end, didn't it? But I guess I must grudgingly thank Mrs. Light, Mr. Bruneli, and all of those other teachers who drummed such knowledge into my head; for without it, accurate comprehension our language in its written form would be difficult. Whether it is the deciphering of a legal document, a fun read of a fast-paced novel, an inquisitive perusal of a news account, or an in-depth study of the Bible; it turns out that grammar is important. Consider the word 'will'. It can be used as a noun, which refers to a person, place, thing, or action; a verb, which expresses existence, action, or occurrence; or, in one of its other forms such as willed, willful, willing or willingly, it could be an adjective, adverb, or participle (we'll leave those definitions for the linguists!!!). 'Will' could also indicate past, present, or future. Fortunately for us, we generally comprehend the meaning of the word by the context and in everyday language it's fairly obvious if the word is descriptive or active. But for purposes of this discussion, let's look first at how will is used grammatically as a noun in the English language. Once we know that, all of its iterations make even more sense, and we may gain a better comprehension of what God has to say about 'will' in His word.

In 1928, Noah Webster described 'will' as: that faculty of the mind by which we determine either to do or forbear an action, the faculty which is exercised in deciding among two or more objects, which we shall embrace or pursue. The will is directed or influenced by the judgment. The understanding or reason compares different objects, which operate as motives; the judgment determines which is preferable, and the will decides which to pursue. In other words, we reason with respect to the value or importance of things; we then judge which is to be preferred; and we will to take the most valuable.[1]

It should be noted that while these are actions commonly thought of as originating from the intellect or soul of man, they may also occur out of the spirit; and, since we are created in God's image, they mirror His capacity for reason, judgment, and will. That man has a will is evident in scripture:

> *Which of the two did the will of his father? They said to Him, "The first."[2]*

> *So then it is not of him who wills, nor of him who runs, but of God who shows mercy.[3]*

> *For a bishop must be blameless, as a steward of God, not self-willed, not quick tempered, not given to wine, not violent, not greedy for money.[4]*

> *For prophecy never came by the will of man, but holy men of God spoke as they were moved by the Holy Spirit.[5]*

> *Do not deliver me to the will of my adversaries; For false witnesses have risen against me, And such as breathe out violence.[6]*

God's will is referenced repeatedly:

> *For whoever does the will of God is My brother and My sister and mother.[7]*

> *Now he who searches the hearts knows what the mind of the Spirit is, because He makes intercession for the saints according to the will of God.[8]*

> *And do not be conformed to this world, but be transformed by the renewing of your mind, that you may prove what is that good and acceptable and perfect will of God.[9]*

> *Not with eyeservice, as men pleasers, but as bondservants of Christ, doing the will of God from the heart.[10]*

'Will' can have to do with disposition, inclination, or desire; and we need to pray, as in the Lord's Prayer:

> *Our Father in heaven, Hallowed be Your name. Your kingdom come. Your will be done On earth as it is in heaven.*[11]

We should also seek His will as Jesus did in the Garden of Gethsemane as He withdrew and:

> *...knelt down and prayed, saying, "Father, if it is Your will, take this cup away from Me; nevertheless not My will, but Yours, be done."*[12]

We've all seen cartoon representations of a person with an angel on one shoulder and a devil on the other, each working to influence the will of the individual. Funny, yes; but also a good illustration of the ongoing battle we face between good and bad choices, choices of will. Out of an act of their will Adam and Eve set the precedent, becoming the first example of the consequences of the ungodly use of free will. Willfully choosing to eat the fruit that God had forbidden resulted not only in their expulsion from the Garden but also in the curse of death upon all whom would follow.[13] Much later, the Pharisees and lawyers rejected the will of God for themselves,[14] and Jesus denounced their evil acts, describing them as hypocrites and declaring seven woes upon them.[15]

We can emulate the will of God or the will of evil; and we should be aware that with ungodly choices come devastating consequences, while Godly choices reap a multitude of blessings:

> *Now therefore, amend your ways and your doings, and obey the voice of the LORD your God; then the LORD will relent concerning the doom that He has pronounced against you.*[16]

> *And the world is passing away, and the lust of it; but he who does the will of God abides forever.*[17]

> *For you have need of endurance, so that after you have done the will of God you may receive the promise: "For yet a little while, And He who is coming will come and will not tarry."*[18]

OK, so man has a will, God has a will, we each have a choice, and it is clear that we are to follow His will rather than our own; but how do we know what that is? Sometimes we can make the process of determining God's will a very difficult thing; at least I know I have. How many times have I agonized over the question, "What is God's will for my life?" More than I can count, but God is faithful. He doesn't leave us floundering around with no answers. When we look to His word and internalize its truth, determining His will becomes much easier. God has not only given us the Bible as an instruction manual, but He has also illustrated it with real-life illustrations regarding how to do things (or not!), and all we have to do is read and follow His directions. We can choose to be confused and frustrated like the stereotypical image of a parent who refuses to read the instructions before putting a toy together at the last minute on Christmas Eve, ending up with a disaster. Or, we can imitate one who sets aside plenty of time, studies the instructions, follows them step-by-step, and assembles the perfect gift in a fraction of the time.

Can it really be that easy? It sounds too simple; just follow God's how-to manual. But we ask, what about this? And what about that? How do I know where to go and what to do next? How do I choose the perfect mate? How do I deal with my bills, my health, my spouse, my kids? Life is not easy; in fact, it's hard; and learning to live by faith can be a challenge. A determination of our will is required to conform to the truth of God's word. For example, I'm absolutely certain that Jesus meant it when He said:

> *Seek first the kingdom of God and His righteousness, and all these things shall be added to you. Therefore do not worry about tomorrow, for tomorrow will worry about its own things. Sufficient for the day is its own trouble.*[19]

Yet, we often willfully choose to ignore His direction and worry about this, that, or whatever.

We still ask, "How can I know His will?" Consider this—all of us experience times when we simply know what our spouse or child or best friend is thinking without them saying a word. It happens because we are so close and know them so well that words are often unnecessary. It's pretty much the same with God; the more intimate we become with Him, the more we know what He's thinking. Our spirits become so attuned to the Holy Spirit that we learn to sense His will in any given situation. It may appear as hesitancy or dread if we're about to make a mistake; as a sense of lightness and freedom if we're on the right path; or any number of other ways in which He chooses to communicate. In Christian circles we may hear this referred to either as a 'check' or a 'hit' in one's spirit.

It's not always easy to move ahead in faith without knowing what comes next, but determining to walk by faith and not by sight is an act of our will that the Lord loves. I submit that life not only falls into place much easier, but also becomes a lot less stressful when He becomes our first priority. Just try it; take a leap of faith!

Look at this account from the Apostle Paul (previously known as Saul):

> *Then a certain Ananias...came to me; and he stood and said to me, 'Brother Saul, receive your sight.' And at that same hour I looked up at him. Then he said, 'The God of our fathers has chosen you that you should know His will, and see the Just One, and hear the voice of His mouth. For you will be His witness to all men of what you have seen and heard. And now why are you waiting? Arise and be baptized, and wash away your sins, calling on the name of the Lord.*[20]

It's pretty clear that Saul's knowledge about God's will was to grow out of a relationship with Jesus; he simply needed to willfully pursue and obey Him. Obviously he heeded that instruction, for it is Paul who later wrote to the Ephesians:

> *In Him we have redemption through His blood...having made known to us the mystery of His will, according to His good pleasure.*

It's also pretty clear that learning to know God's will didn't necessarily come overnight for Paul any more than it does for us. Writing to the Galatians, he said:

> *But when it pleased God...to reveal His Son in me, that I might preach Him among the Gentiles, I did not immediately confer with*

flesh and blood, nor did I go up to Jerusalem to those who were apostles before me; but I went to Arabia, and returned again to Damascus. Then after three years I went up to Jerusalem.[21]

Three years! Are any among us willing to seek Him first non-stop for that long in order to know His will?

God's will is revealed in His Son; and Jesus Himself said:

If anyone wills to do His will, he shall know concerning the doctrine, whether it is from God or whether I speak on My own authority.[22]

The more we study the life of Jesus and the better we get to know Him, the easier it is to determine the will of God. It starts with redemption; it continues with relationship; it is evidenced by the choices we make out of our will. And once again the Apostle Paul offers some great advice regarding how to proceed:

Rejoice in the Lord always. Again I will say, rejoice! Let your gentleness be known to all men. The Lord is at hand. Be anxious for nothing, but in everything by prayer and supplication, with thanksgiving, let your requests be made known to God; and the peace of God, which surpasses all understanding, will guard your hearts and minds through Christ Jesus. Finally, brethren, whatever things are true, whatever things are noble, whatever things are just, whatever things are pure, whatever things are lovely, whatever things are of good report, if there is any virtue and if there is anything praiseworthy— meditate on these things.[23]

But it gets even better. 'Will' may also refer to a legal document that dictates the disposition of an estate; and:

The Spirit Himself bears witness with our spirit that we are children of God, and if children, then heirs—heirs of God and joint heirs with Christ, if indeed we suffer with Him, that we may also be glorified together.[24]

In Him also we have obtained an inheritance.[25]

According to His will, He has willed us an unparalleled inheritance.

Finally, we are the recipients of an amazing promise, with will appearing as an auxiliary verb signifying the future tense:

> *He who overcomes, I will make him a pillar in the temple of My God, and he shall go out no more. I will write on him the name of My God and the name of the city of My God, the New Jerusalem, which comes down out of heaven from My God. And I will write on him My new name.*[26]

[1] Webster, Noah. (1928). *American Dictionary of the English Language.* (Facsimile Edition 1967). Chesapeake, Virginia: Foundation for American Christian Education

[2] Matthew 21:31a

[3] Romans 9:16

[4] Titus 1:7

[5] 2 Peter 4:19

[6] Psalm 27:12

[7] Mark 3:35

[8] Romans 8:27

[9] Romans 12:2

[10] Ephesians 6:6

[11] Matthew 6:9-10

[12] Luke 20:41-42

[13] Genesis 3

[14] Luke 7:30

[15] Matthew 23

[16] Jeremiah 26:13

[17] Hebrews 10:36-37

[18] Matthew 6:33-34

[19] Acts 22:12-16

[20] Ephesians 1:7, 9

[21] Galatians 1:15-18

[22] John 7:17

[23] Philippians 4:4-8

[24] Romans 8:16-17

[25] Ephesians 1:11a

[26] Revelation 3:12

CHAPTER ELEVEN
INTRODUCTION TO THE WIDTH, LENGTH, DEPTH, AND HEIGHT

In November 2011, my friend Rob Gross and I (Paul) were enjoying an evening meal at our hotel restaurant in Hong Kong when, unexpectedly, we started discerning something new. We agreed that we did not know what it was, so we started asking the Lord a series of who-or-what questions, receiving no positive results; but then we were startled to understand that we were both discerning the archangel Michael. I heard in my spirit, "Daniel 12," and my first inclination was that there was nothing about Michael in that passage. Looking it up, though, we were surprised that the archangel Michael is indeed mentioned in the first verse. Why were we discerning Michael? Was there some clue in Daniel 12 that would give us insight?

Daniel 12 is about the end of days and the sealing of the scrolls of Daniel, and the 9th verse indicates that they will not be opened until the time of the end. Are we now in those last days? Are Daniel's sealed scrolls finally being unsealed and released? If so, what is this new revelation the Lord desires us to understand? At that evening meal it seemed that these questions had no answers, but that would soon change as the Lord began unlocking more and more mysteries of the Kingdom of God.

The Lord had started speaking to us about the depth in general terms in 2006, but within a few years the words became more and more specific until 2009 when we wrote the *Prayer to Release One From the Ungodly Depth* at a ministry school. At that time we did not realize that the Lord had not only begun to give us understanding about the depth, but also about the width, length, and height. That new revelation would come after our time in Hong Kong.

The width, length, depth, and height are mentioned in Ephesians in the context of a prayer of Apostle Paul:

> *For this reason I bow my knees to the Father of our Lord Jesus Christ, from whom the whole family in heaven and earth is named, that He would grant you, according to the riches of His glory, to be strengthened with might through His Spirit in the inner man, that Christ may dwell in your hearts through faith; that you, being rooted and grounded in love, may be able to comprehend with all the saints what is the width and length and depth and height—to know the love of Christ which passes knowledge; that you may be filled with all the fullness of God.*[1]

Only the depth and height are mentioned in Romans 8:38-39:

> *For I am persuaded that neither death nor life, nor angels nor principalities nor powers, nor things present nor things to come, nor height nor depth, nor any other created thing, shall be able to separate us from the love of God which is in Christ Jesus our Lord.*

What do we understand about the width, length, depth, and height? As a Baptist pastor I consulted as many commentaries as possible to obtain insight into a passage of scripture, so in preparation for this chapter I thought it would be helpful to search out this matter in that way. The consensus is quickly apparent—no one seems to know what the width, length, depth, and height are. Quotes from three commentaries are representative of what commentators are saying:

- We are not intended to give detailed meanings to *the breadth and length and height and depth*; rather we are to feel with heart and mind and intuition the 'many dimensions' of love, and work to weave that love into all the fabric of life.[2]

- It is not directly designated, and hence must be taken from the context. The added clause connected with this by points at once to 'the love of Christ.' The dimensions set forth here then become clear: 'breadth' refers to the nations lying beside each other on the earth, over all of whom the love of Christ will extend itself; 'length,' to the successive ages during which it will reach; 'depth,' to the misery and corruption of sin, into which it will descend; 'height' to the glory at God's throne and near His heart to which it would elevate all.[3]

- No special interpretations are to be given to these words. The general idea of vastness is expressed in these ordinary terms for dimension. Notice that the article is attached only to the first, 'breadth', all the rest being included under the one article; the intention being to exhibit the love of Christ in its entire dimension, and not to fix the mind on its constituent parts.[4]

Having determined that even the experts do not know much about width, length, depth, and height, I decided we could at least look at the context of Ephesians 3:18 and define it by the surrounding passage. The verse is in a prayer of the Apostle Paul, uttered on behalf of the Ephesians. In the larger context of Ephesians 3 we notice several statements that would indicate what Paul links together with the width, length, depth and height.

Mysteries of Christ:

> *(...by which, when you read, you may understand my knowledge in the mystery of Christ), which in other ages was not made known to the sons of men, as it has now been revealed by the Spirit to His holy apostles and prophets...and to make all see what is the fellowship of the mystery, which from the beginning of the ages has been hidden in God who created all things through Jesus Christ; to the intent that now the manifold wisdom of God might be made known by the church to the principalities and powers in the heavenly places, according to the eternal purpose which He accomplished in Christ Jesus our Lord.[5]*

Evangelism:

> *...that the Gentiles should be fellow heirs, of the same body, and partakers of His promise in Christ through the gospel.[6]*

Perseverance in trials:

> *Therefore I ask that you do not lose heart at my tribulations for you, which is your glory.[7]*

Strengthening of the inner man:

...that He would grant you, according to the riches of His glory, to be strengthened with might through His Spirit in the inner man.[8]

The love of Christ:

...to know the love of Christ which passes knowledge; that you may be filled with all the fullness of God.[9]

The working of god's power:

Now to Him who is able to do exceedingly abundantly above all that we ask or think, according to the power that works in us...[10]

Unity:

I therefore, the prisoner of the Lord, beseech you to walk worthy of the calling with which you were called, with all lowliness and gentleness, with longsuffering, bearing with one another in love, endeavoring to keep the unity of the Spirit in the bond of peace. There is one body and one Spirit, just as you were called in one hope of your calling; one Lord, one faith, one baptism; one God and Father of all, who is above all, and through all, and in you all.[11]

Spiritual gifts:

But to each one of us grace was given according to the measure of Christ's gift.[12]

This is the end of what we can intellectually conclude about the width, length, depth, and height; and we are exactly at the place the Lord wants us to be—totally dependent on Him to give understanding and wisdom. We must depend on Him for the revelation of these mysteries. It is now time for the Holy Spirit to reveal the secrets about the width, length, depth, and height.

[1] Ephesians 3:14-19

[2] Foulkes, F. (1989). *Ephesians: an Introduction and Commentary* (Vol. 10, p. 111). Downers Grove, IL: InterVarsity Press.

[3] Lange, J. P., Schaff, P., Braune, K., & Riddle, M. B. (2008). *A Commentary on the Holy Scriptures* (p. 126). Bellingham, WA: Logos Bible Software.

[4] Vincent, M. R. (1887). *Word Studies in the New Testament* (Vol. 3, p. 385). New York: Charles Scribner's Sons.

[5] Ephesians 3:4-5, 9-11

[6] Ephesians 3:6

[7] Ephesians 3:13

[8] Ephesians 3:16

[9] Ephesians 3:19

[10] Ephesians 3:20

[11] Ephesians 4:1–6

[12] Ephesians 4:7

CHAPTER TWELVE
DISCOVERING THE DEPTH

When we publish a new prayer people often ask, "When did you write the prayer?" I (Paul) do not write the prayers; they are written in our gatherings as a cooperative effort of all of the people present. Virtually all of the revelation we have received has started with me receiving some sort of spark, such as a dream, impression, or word from someone else; which was then fleshed out and developed in a group.

In 2006, a prayer minister had a dream in which I was talking to her from heaven. She saw a grid and was instructed to go in and disconnect something. I said, "You have to be a minor." Then another prayer minister asked her, "Are you a minor?" She replied, "No, I am over 21." "Then you can't go in."

Later, she had a vision in which she had a yellow helmet with lights like a miner's hat. She was to dig for the answers. She got the word, "Cash in, cash in, there are veins of gold that need to be uncovered", and realized that it was not a 'minor' in terms of being under 21, but a 'miner' to dig into the depths. Two years later in 2008, still with no understanding of the meaning of the depth, two different intercessors gave me words associated with it.

> (First word) It is now. Paul, Paul, we give you authority to tear down the strongholds. Find the keys beneath the ground; go deep, deep, deep; they are underneath. You are going to uncover the enemy's strategy, the hiding place of the enemy, just like a miner [I had heard that before!]. Go underground and dig deep, it is there. Numbers, strategies, ledgers have been hidden. You will tear down more financial strongholds. It is time; it is time that finances are released. There are vaults. You will be given the combination. When you open up the vaults, information is going to come gushing out.

> (Second word) It is a new living day; it is going to be

different; it is going to be fun. [I like that part.] It gives the King pleasure for you to wait it out. It is new; it is living; it is alive; it is waiting. In the quietness you will find it. In the Holy Place you will find it. Father, we bow down before You, for You are the Holy One. The Establisher has come again; this is God. There is a new living way. I will break your old ways of doing things, seeing things, hearing things. Expectancy; without it you are not going to get there. When expectancy meets Jesus, who is Love, then expectancy is fulfilled. When expectancy has reached its fullness of time, then birth takes place. The beginning becomes the end, which becomes the beginning and old things are passed away.

I then remembered a dream I'd had. I was in Manhattan, and found myself in a warehouse district at the end of a railroad line. There was a well and I reached into it and pulled my grandson, who was born with cystic hygroma, out by his hair. Instantly he was healed. Was this the depth?

We have been told for a long time that we must go higher; we must go higher; we must go higher. But now the Lord was clearly saying, "You must go deeper; you must go deeper; you must go deeper. You must know the deep things of God which are not in the height, but they are in the depth." We suddenly found ourselves on a new frontier of knowledge. This revelation of the depth has opened new realms for personal healing. What is the depth?

CHAPTER THIRTEEN
PLACES IN THE DEPTH

A pastor had come for ministry and an intercessor saw him in a cave under water. He appeared to be confined within a clear glass cube, and the Lord showed us that he was trapped in the ungodly depth in Sheol. I (Paul) could feel the cube, and he acknowledged that he had felt trapped throughout most of his life. The Lord led us to ask Him to release the man from Sheol. We did, and the immediate change in this man was remarkable. He was overcome by a sense of relief.

Following the prayer session I received a call from my daughter, Corrie. She had just returned from a doctor's appointment because of severe abdominal pain. The doctor did a sonogram and discovered that she had a cyst. Loaded with this new revelation about the depth, I traveled to her home and asked the Lord to take her out of the ungodly depth. The next day after another visit to the doctor for more tests, I received a call from my excited daughter. "Dad, I'm healed." I said, "What?" She replied that they'd taken another sonogram and could not find the cyst. The Lord was confirming that this new revelation was not only true but also very important.

The revelation of the depth has been one of the most profound revelations the Lord has given us, as well as one of the most difficult to receive and believe. I remember so clearly when the revelation was coming that I found myself in disbelief that the insights were true. At one point an intercessor was giving a word from the Lord when she turned to me and said, "The Lord says 'stop being so religious and listen to me.'" I was shocked by the comment but opened my spirit and mind to truly listen.

So often in this journey I am forced to take a leap of faith, re-examine the Bible, and walk out what the Lord is revealing. That has been difficult. However, as ministry takes place and people's lives are changed, faith turns to true belief. I am constantly aware that I want to see true results in people's lives; I want to see changes that bring new levels of freedom and a closer walk with the Lord. The revelation of the depth has accomplished this; and yes, it is Biblical, so we will explore this truth. First, however, please consider the testimony of a life that was dramatically altered through prayer as passages about the depth as principles from the Word of God were applied. Pastor Rob Gross of Kaneohe, Hawaii, contributes this wonderful story.

> In 2010, I met with a concerned grandmother and her granddaughter for a prayer counseling session. The grandmother, as the girl's legal guardian, shared that the she had been taken from her mother because of severe physical and verbal abuse. This included being hit under her throat with a clothes hanger and having a cabinet door smashed on her head after the mother had ripped it off its hinges in a fit of rage. The girl's father was in prison.
>
> Diagnosed with bi-polar syndrome, this cute ten-year-old was having a difficult time getting along with her teacher and classmates. During the session the girl shared that her deepest hurt stemmed from being separated from her two younger sisters because of her mother's abuse. It was obvious that she was trapped in the ungodly depths.
>
> After praying to be set free from the ungodly depths, the two left encouraged. A month later I was informed by the grandmother that her granddaughter no longer suffered from bi-polar syndrome and was doing much better in school. And today, her fourteen-year-old granddaughter continues to thrive and has a bright future.

There is one relevant Hebrew word that is translated as 'depth', is *ameq* (adjective) or *omeq* (noun), and it is found twice in Proverbs:

> *But he does not know that the dead are there, That her guests are in the depths (ameq) of hell [Sheol].* [1]

> *As the heavens for height and the earth for depth, (omeq) So the heart of kings is unsearchable.* [2]

In these passages, as well as others in the Old Testament, there seems to be a linking of the Hebrew word for 'depth' with Sheol, which is known as Hades in the New Testament. This place in the depth would be the unrighteous location of soul parts.

Previously, as a Baptist pastor, I would teach on Sheol as a place where the dead, righteous and unrighteous, remained until the coming of the Messiah, believing that they would be transferred to either heaven or hell at that time. As the revelation continued about the depth, I came to understand that Sheol is a place where parts of us can be trapped because either others or we have put them there. I realize this sounds bizarre so I will continue to explain.

As we began to explore the depth, the Lord upgraded our armor, for it appears we need greater protection there. It is very strange, but the new set of armor feels like I am enveloped in humidity and it is clammy. There is also a ringing in my ears, and others have experienced the same sensation. As we enter the depth, it feels as if we are going down. The Lord began speaking a new word to us about what we were experiencing:

> (Prayer Minister) It is a different type of suit; it's a miner suit [the miner again!], miner gear. Put it into the car, like a mineshaft car. Dig; dig deep. There are tools down there. I am transporting you through time and space. Take the tools and take the equipment. There is more depth to learn. You have only scratched the surface. There is more, more, more. There is gold in these veins. Mine the gold; mine the treasure, not the treasure—revelation. You will bring it back to the surface; coming up; you will take this back. [He was putting inside of us a lightning rod, a shaft of light inside of each of us.] You will reflect and seek His light; you will speak His light; you will taste His light; you will know His light. Transverse the light.

> (Paul Cox) Yahweh, Yahweh; you are all builders; you are makers with Yahweh as co-creators. Your wealth, your treasure has not been rejected. Miners, miners, you must be a miner for the heart of gold. There is a fine line between heart and mind. Where is your hope stored? What is it for? Heart and mind are to become builders and makers, a co-

creator. It is time to find the time to know, hear, and believe; taste and see; you become a miner for a heart of gold. Buy gold refined in fire. Heal the heart; heal the mind; heal the man; heal the land. Dig deeper; come up higher, to be a miner for the heart of gold.

In 2009, we were in Collingwood, Canada, when a prophet delivered another relevant word about the depth:

We are now at the bottom of the ocean. It is about a mindset. If we only dwell in the mindset of the river, we stay in our own personal anointing. We need to move out into the ocean, which is the depth, lose our lives and surrender all, enter in and cross over into the mindset of the ocean, and we will have the mind of Christ. If we only dwell in the mindset of the river we will lose what is in the depth. Enter into the mindset of the ocean; you will have the mind of Christ. It is the voice of many waters. It is the voice of many waters coming forth from the depth of the ocean, from the mind of Christ, not from the mind of man.

It is time to come out of the river and go into the ocean. It is time for the mind of the ocean. It is time for the ocean liner. No longer time for personal ministries and empires. Personal ministries, empires, and anointing will be submerged. Have I not given dreams of the tsunami? I am the tsunami. You will never figure me out. Why do you lean on your own understanding to figure Me out? Your natural man cannot comprehend the things of the Father. Your thoughts are not My thoughts; your ways are not My ways. It is time to bow low so that He might be lifted high. Your thoughts are not My ways. I am bringing forth a depth of Me, a depth of Me. I will be the tsunami of great glory and great power to and through My yielded bride and sons.

[The hirelings are being fired. The sons and daughters will rise with a depth of God in their eyes. Is there a depth of our souls that are not? He is trying to rewire the house from 110 to 220, Galatians 2:20, no longer I but Christ.]

Acknowledge that you are dead. Why would you die daily when you are dead? Choose to obey the word and take up the cross daily. I have baptized you into the depths. Quit trying to die when you are dead in me. I went to the depths to take you into My depths. Record yourself dead for He has done it. Not by might, but My Spirit. As in the days of Noah there was a flood, I will flood the earth with re and renewing fire. There is a renewing and restoring fire. I will judge evil. I will restore and bring back the garden. I will bring back your identity in glory. As it was in the beginning, it will also be on earth again. Bring back the depth of the garden. I will split forth the Adamic way of the mind of men. I will split and divide asunder that which is tares and wheat so that out of the depth comes the redeemed, the last Adam, the redeemed, the One New Man. Mark this day, heaven and earth will witness, holy congregation. This day in the Spirit something is being recorded; a recording in heaven. In the depth is deeper revelation, deeper commitment, deeper love."

In 2009, we also got the word:

I show you a mystery. The hidden depths of God are here, the mystery of the power of God of ages long ago. The hidden mysteries created long ago. There is a mystery of knowing Him face-to-face in the origin. Deeper still, there is a hidden treasure to be revealed.

There is freedom when we are moved out of the ungodly depth and great release into the purposes of God when we are positioned in the righteous depth. David expressed the promise of Scripture:

That I would see the goodness of the LORD in the land of the living.[3]

Next, we move from the general to the specific; from an overview of the ungodly depth to a specific understanding of the locations in the ungodly depth; we discover what it means to enjoy the privilege of the freedom of our soul in the righteous depth.

[1] Proverbs 9:18
[2] Proverbs 25:3
[3] Psalm 27:13

CHAPTER FOURTEEN
EXPLORING THE DEPTH

We had discovered that there are many places in the depth, but the Lord wasn't finished pouring out revelation.

An intercessor received a poem that is tied completely to this, a Dr. Seuss sort of thing:

> There is a star, a star upon Thars, which gives off light both near and far.
>
> Dimensions it knows throwing beams, oh so far, yes it circles and circles both near and so far.
>
> It appears as the darkness bringing light from above, setting free the captives, captives from birth, giving them freedom, new hope, and new birth.
>
> It shatters walls, glass partitions, and more.
>
> It opens up portals and heavenlies too, for My grace to pour in afresh and anew.
>
> It rearranges vibrations and it clarifies sounds, bringing healing and health as it resounds.

A prayer minister had another dream:

> I go into the ocean to swim [the depth]. The water is so shallow and I search for deeper water and cannot find it. I swim parallel to the beach and then I swim opposite the beach, going out as far as I could, looking for deeper water. I finally hit a plastic wall and find that I am in a movie set. The ocean is not real but manmade, and there is no depth or width. I hit a plastic wall that was painted to look like it went into the distance.

Realizing that the Lord was giving a revelation of Sheol, we examined several scriptures:

> *All of his sons and all of his daughters rose to comfort him, but he refused to be comforted so he was very sad and said, "For I shall go down to the grave [that is really to Sheol] in mourning."*[1] (This refers to Jacob.)

> *The wicked shall be turned into hell [Sheol], And all the nations that forget God.*[2]

> *O LORD, You brought my soul up from the grave [Sheol]; You have kept me alive, that I should not go down to the pit.*[3]

I (Paul) wondered, "Is a person trapped in Sheol or the pit?" So, in a meeting, I asked for a volunteer to illustrate through exploration and discovered that I could discern an individual in a cube, trapped in Sheol. Remember, in the dream it felt like reality but was just a movie set, and the interpretation reveals that your actual reality is not the reality that God has for you. Let me say that again. The actual reality that you are experiencing is not the reality that God has for you. You are in an artificial reality.

Next, I discerned another cube with an ungodly elder standing guard, followed by another cube with an ungodly ruler—a cube in a cube in a cube, keeping people trapped in Sheol.

Let me summarize. Let's say someone comes and criticizes me and I buy into the criticism. At that point I get put into Sheol or into the pit because I have accepted the untruth that has been spoken about me. Also, by the words they speak, people can put you there even if you don't agree. The realization came that the experience in the church when the membership came against me violently resulted in me being put into dark places in Sheol, and the pit especially.

I have come to believe that this is the place where the enemy grabs parts of us and attacks parts of other people. It is the place where all sorts of condemnation, guilt, shame, and rejection is being empowered because we are multidimensional people. We are seated with Christ in heavenly places, and we exist in lots of places (dimensions). Notice the Biblical emphasis is plural—heavenly places. What's happening is that there are people who exist in an ungodly depth where the enemy is using them against you, so you are constantly bombarded with thoughts that are not correct. Does that make any sense? As it happens over and over again and you wonder, "Why do I feel like this?" Sometimes you may even come up to people you've never met and immediately dislike them. You see something going on in the depths is affecting you. We are meant to be in the Godly depths, which I believe are the depths of revelation.

I checked for cubes on a couple of teenagers and found that they were not trapped, so it seems very interesting that scripture talks about old age in Sheol. I think what happens is that there is a point in life where we stop dreaming and we start buying into the lies that this is all there is. We start accepting untruths that are being spoken about us. At some point, I don't know when but probably somewhere in the 20s or 30s, we end up being placed into the ungodly depths. We've come to a time in which we believe that we have experienced all life has to offer; we buy into the lie.

We have discerned that the snare and the trap are actual places in the depth, as is the pit, which appears to be layered. It actually says in one verse that you go into the depth, the deepest part of Sheol, so there appear to be layers.[4]

> Let their table become a snare before them, And their well-being a trap.[5]

> The proud have hidden a snare for me, and cords; They have spread a net by the wayside; They have set traps for me. Selah[6]

> Keep me from the snares they have laid for me, And from the traps of the workers of iniquity.[7]

I have found that traps can be discerned on the feet. Keep in mind that a trap is different than a snare; it's like a bear trap, while a snare is a piece of string in which you snare the leg or the neck of a bird. When we discern traps and snares we just pray, "Lord, we remove the snare and the trap off of him. Lord, would You remove him out of those places in the ungodly depth?" And He does; we can no longer sense them. You can do the same thing now; pray, "Lord Jesus, would You now remove the snare off of me, the trap off of me, and take me out of the pit?"

In New Jersey, I had a sense that the person to whom I was ministering, a woman with dissociative identity disorder, was in a cage. It felt like two ping- pong balls were circling above my head, but I did not know what that meant. Meanwhile, someone was upstairs praying and they reported that they saw the person in a birdcage, exactly as I had discerned. I realized that the Lord was telling me that I was feeling celestial beings, and since then have discerned them many, many times. When I feel righteous celestial beings, it feels like three Ping-Pong balls circling my head, like when they draw the lottery with those balls flying around. Some have seen the celestial beings as resembling an atom.

Celestial beings are mentioned in Jude 1:8:

> *Likewise also these dreamers de le the flesh, reject authority, and speak evil of dignitaries.*

The dignitaries are really the 'doxas', which means the glorious ones or, in another translation, celestial beings. I asked the Lord what this meant and His answer was wonderful—I love this! The celestial beings are living light rays; light is a living being; and they are the glorious ones. Remember the story about Moses in which his face shone and they had to put a veil over it? In the Hebrew it actually means that he had laser-like rays coming off his face, and those are the glorious ones, the living light beings.

So we asked the Lord the question, "How do we get out of Sheol?" He said to us, "You must go through the star and follow the glorious ones. They will go into the ungodly depth and take you out and set you free."

Backtracking a bit let me tell you of a vision an intercessor had for me. Keep in mind that this was before we had any information about the depth. She said, "You are walking across a bridge, like the Golden Gate Bridge. The Lord said, 'You can keep on walking and you will continue, and you will be alright; or you can jump.'" I said, "Well, I'll jump. That's simple." I did not realize at the time that when you jump you go into the depth. So now, in our meetings, if the glorious ones are present we take a leap of faith and jump by praying the following prayer. Then, we may wait awhile as deliverance takes place:

> *Lord Jesus, I repent for accepting the evaluation of others, for allowing others to determine where I should be.*

> *Lord, I realize that this has happened in my generational line also, but I declare that I want to see You in the land of the living. I am tired of living the way I have been living.*

> *Lord, I follow now Your glorious ones through the star into the ungodly depths. Would You pull every part of me out of the ungodly depths, out of Sheol, out of the pit, out of the outer darkness, out of death, and out of any other place in the ungodly depth?*

> *I declare that I will be seated with Christ in heavenly places. I will be seated in the Godly width, the Godly length, the Godly height, and the Godly depth. I will be a revealed son of the Most High God. I will take my place as the One New Man with Christ as the Head.*

Fear is another place we have discerned in the ungodly depth, so we also ask the Lord to take us out of fear, and afterward we have discerned that the cubes are gone.

Let me be brutally honest here. If this has worked, then you will notice a difference. Remember, with my daughter it was something we could measure. Something should change in your mood, your outlook; in the way you view life; there should be something tangible that happens. If this works, I believe it happens generationally as well.

When we first began discovering Sheol, as we were talking about the depth we all got our suits on and went into the depth. When a person had a vision of his family line in Sheol, I wondered if we were getting into some kinky theology. But then he said something very interesting, "I see both the righteous (the redeemed) and the unredeemed there." So I wondered, "If these are really parts of us, is it possible that some of these parts could still be in Sheol?"

When we are absent from the body, we are where? Present with the Lord.[8] So while it appears that our line somehow can be trapped there, I don't know what it all means. I believe that while we are not rescuing our ancestors from Sheol, something has happened in our generational line because I can discern a difference after we pray; something we have yet to comprehend.

Why would we go through this exercise? Because there is always more. There actually are treasures in the darkness. There are treasures and gold in the veins. I think there are finances; I believe there is revelation; and this may be tied to the unsealing of scrolls mentioned in Daniel 12.

As we continue to explore the depths, we will also explore the heights, the lengths, and the widths. The Lord keeps saying to us that we have only just begun. This is a great adventure; and if I have done nothing else, I hope that I have unlocked the possibility that there is more. For we who are Christians, there is always more. For kids, a lifetime in which they will never get bored because they are discovering more and more and more about God. Isn't that great?

Our desire is to know the width, the length, the height, and the depth of God; believing that He will give us wisdom and understanding so that we might know Him better; gaining ever increasing freedom.

In the '80s there was a television show that I really liked, *Sea Quest*. I started re-watching it shortly before the Lord started this revelation. So now we have *Star Trek*, which is the heavenly places, and *Sea Quest*, which goes into the deep.

Lord, we want to go on a *Sea Quest* and on a *Star Trek*. We want to explore the universes, the outer universes, and the universes in the depth. Holy Spirit, please fill every place now that has been vacated by enemy entrapment, and work in our minds and hearts to teach us about the deep things of God.

[1] Genesis 37:35
[2] Psalm 9:17
[3] Psalm 30:3
[4] Deuteronomy 22:32
[5] Psalm 69:22
[6] Psalm 140:5
[7] Psalm 141:9
[8] 1 Corinthians 5:8

CHAPTER FIFTEEN
PRAYER TO RELEASE ONE FROM THE UNGODLY DEPTH

Father, I repent and renounce for myself and my family line for all sins that have kept me bound and unable to fulfill my God-given purpose and that have carried the consequence of entrapment in the ungodly depth, Sheol, the pit, the snare, and the trap.

Father, have mercy on me, for I have endured much contempt and ridicule. Lord, break off the contempt and ridicule that has been put on me by the proud. Wash me from the arrogance and arrogant ways that brought the contempt upon me.

Lord, forgive me for not forgiving those who have come against me and entrapped me. I choose now to forgive those who have spoken contempt against me, and release them to you.

I repent for and renounce vows, covenants, and promises to You and to others, which I broke. Please cancel and break off any evil or ungodly consequences of these broken vows, covenants, and promises.

I choose to cancel and forgive all broken vows, covenants, and promises made by others to me and to members of my generational line. I trust Your words that You will repay, and now choose to forgive them freely and release them.

I repent for all those who forgot or turned away from You; and for all who, even though they saw Your awesome works, were ungrateful and unthankful, complaining instead of thanking and being grateful for all You have done. Please break off these consequences.

I repent for all those in my generational line who tried to ascend above the stars or above God.

I repent for all generational fear, especially the fear of man, and for all who ran from fear, thus causing them to fall into the pit.

I repent for all who caused conflict, strife, or disunity, especially in the body of Christ.

I repent for pride, arrogance, deceit, anger and fury, generational adultery, harlotry, immorality, sexual perversion, ungodly bloodshed, murdering of the innocent; and for using ungodly seduction, enticement, or allurement to lead the upright and the righteous astray.

I repent for all who had foolish lips and did not watch the words of their mouths.

I repent for all who cursed father or mother.

I repent for hatred, racism, and slavery; and for putting others in the ungodly depth by hating, despising, and discriminating based on skin color, culture, gender, and beliefs.

I also choose to forgive those who came against my family line for these reasons. Lord, break the consequences of these sins off my family line; restore love that goes beyond racial, cultural, economic, gender, and diversity boundaries. Please remove me and my lamp from any ungodly secret place, and from the deep darkness.

Lord, please release me from any ungodly contracts that have brought my ancestors or me into the spirit of poverty. Please redeem what the devil has taken away and restore Your riches and Your glory.

I renounce all generational curses that come with seeking worldly riches. Please cause me to seek riches in You alone. I repent for robbing the poor, swindling, gambling, cheating, and using witchcraft to gain wealth, and for all greedy gain of wealth, power, knowledge, titles, position, mantles, and wisdom from ungodly sources.

I repent for myself and all who were destroyed through lack of knowledge because they did not seek You, Your knowledge, and Your wisdom; for all who did not seek Your guidance in their walk, business, work, ministry, family, or other circles of influence. Please remove my family and ministry from any ungodly depth, pit, trap, or snare. Please restore to me all the blessings and benefits that have been held in the ungodly depth for my family line.

I declare that the enemy will now fall into the trap and snare he had set for me.

I repent for all who did not walk in true spiritual unity, but allowed bitterness, jealousy, and envy that caused us to fall into a trap and a snare; for all who did not guard friends, family, or the Body of Christ, and watched them fall into ungodly depths.

I repent for casting an evil eye on others because of envy and jealousy, thus placing them into ungodly depths. Please remove and restore any parts of me that were placed in ungodly depths due to the evil eye.

I repent for all ungodly passivity that has caused me to come into agreement with unjust accusations, ungodly perceptions, ungodly images, word curses, limitations, gossip, and slander against me or against anything that belongs to me. Please disconnect me from all these and cancel them. I now choose to come into agreement with Your perception of me.

Lord, in your mercy please break off any ungodly work of my hands. I repent for allowing myself to be put into the ungodly depths through the worship of foreign gods, idols, and ungodly beings; and especially through drugs and the spirit of pharmakeia. Please remove any part of me that has been trapped in the dimensions and cleanse it in Your blood.

I repent for uttering false prophecies, ungodly prayers, witchcraft curses, or incantations that have placed me into any ungodly depths. Please remove all consequences of these actions.

Lord, please disconnect me from any ungodly physical touch, trauma, or assault that has trapped any part of me in ungodly depths.

I repent for all who committed acts or harbored emotions that would place us into any ungodly depth; and for all dishonest or unjust covenants. I forgive those who committed injustice and brought false accusations against us.

I repent for all fear of man, for not caring for the widows and fatherless, and for declaring that no one would restore us from the pit, Sheol, Hades, or any ungodly depth. I choose to believe and declare that You are the one true God and will restore me.

Lord, please now rescue me and my family line from all places in the ungodly depth that trapped us, and restore us to Your True and Righteous depth and height, Your plumb line.

Father, in Jesus' name, my desire is to be rightly related to You, to have all that You intend to give me, and to receive all of my inheritance. I ask You to open my eyes and correct my perceptions; show me how to work out my salvation daily; show me what to let go of and to whom I should extend forgiveness so my position will change. Lord, I repent for self-righteousness and wrongly judgments against others. Please remove the shackle from my left leg.

I repent for denying miracles, power, and the resurrection that You purchased. Please remove any balls and chains from me; take me out of any whitewashed sepulchers; set me free from the grave.

Lord, please shatter the glass walls of deception and ungodly perceptions that keep me from hearing, speaking, and seeing clearly with Your perception.

I repent for not acknowledging that the sins of my ancestors and their belief systems affect me today. I repent for blind ignorance and passivity that has kept me from taking the kingdom by force. I choose to awaken to righteousness. Please give me a heart of humility and position me rightly before You.

Lord, please fill my heart with Your love and give me a revelation of who You are and how my walk is to appear.

Father God, I repent for putting others, especially brothers and sisters in Christ, into the pit through judgments, selfish ambition, and jealousy; I repent for choosing to live in the victim mentality.

I repent for all idolatry and ungodly worship of man or man's ways, and not truly worshiping and exalting You.

Lord, please disconnect me from the ungodly star and the ungodly elders that are holding and chaining me to the pit; take off the ungodly cummerbund, the knots and cords that have trapped me.

Lord, please break, shatter, destroy, cut off, and remove any witchcraft that has empowered my entrapment in any of these ungodly dimensional places such as Sheol, death, fear, Hades, the snare, ungodly depth, perdition, the pits, the darkest place, utter darkness, or the deep darkness. I repent for all who used seduction or any sexual practice as a means to entice and entrap people into ungodly dimensions.

Lord, remove me from the deep darkness of Sheol, the ungodly depth, fear, the snare, the trap, perdition, the pit, the darkest place, utter darkness, or the deep darkness. Please remove the snares, traps, and nets that have bound my soul, my spirit, my body, and my health in the ungodly depths.

CHAPTER SIXTEEN

INTRODUCTION TO THE PRAYER TO RELEASE THE TREASURES OF DARKNESS

The Prayer to Release One from the Ungodly Depth had just been completed, but it was clear the Lord was not finished with His ongoing revelation. It was apparent that another prayer was being birthed as the Lord spoke to us about financial blessings that had been stopped up because of generational sins. As the revelation owed, I (Paul) was praying about what questions we needed to ask the Lord, because we had already repented for everything we could think of to repent for. A lady sitting next to me had been up all night, praying and seeking the Lord for a solution to our dilemma. Suddenly she spoke the phrase, "Year of Jubilee," and I knew she had provided the solution. We were to repent for all the years of Jubilee that our ancestors had failed to observe. Because debts had not been cancelled, all those in our family line were still paying them off, even as those debts continued to escalate. The enemy had held our lines in financial bondage for many generations.

When we finished the prayer, I sensed that we had done what we were supposed to do but questioned whether it would reap any benefits. I determined that I would not tell anyone about it until I had seen some tangible proof that the prayer actually accomplished the desired goal.

During this time I had been traveling, and when I arrived at the airport to go home I engaged a sky cab to help with my luggage and ticket. Because of the extra media that I was bringing home, I knew that I would have to pay at least $60 in baggage fees to cover the extra weight. The sky cab took the luggage into the terminal and returned with my ticket. I had my wallet out, prepared to pay the fees, but he told me that there would be no charge. I was stunned. I then thanked the Lord for this blessing, but told Him that while I was very grateful I still wanted to see the big deal about the prayer.

I returned home and managed not to tell anyone about the new prayer. A couple of weeks went by and one day while I was at Aslan's Place, Donna called me. It was evident that she was very excited. She told me that a lady had come to our door and given her a very large check. She was told it was not for Aslan's Place or me, but for her; and it was a payment for all what she and her generational line had lost. I was stunned, but was now a believer! The Lord really had led us into a new understanding of how to recover what has been lost in our generational line.

CHAPTER 17

PRAYER TO RELEASE THE
TREASURES OF DARKNESS

Lord, I repent for myself and my ancestors for coming into agreement with Satan and seeking riches at all cost, lusting after our own glory, wealth, and position at the expense of others and future generations.

Lord, I repent for the following sins:

- Receiving and agreeing with the sounds, words, and songs of Satan and for asking him to make us rich and famous no matter the cost

- Lusting after my own glory on this side of eternity, instead of waiting on God to justly, generously, graciously, and extravagantly care for and reward me in this life and the next

- Manipulating sound and words in order to make us look good and come out on top at all costs

- Puffing myself up, instead of seeking to lay down my life for others

- Stealing God's glory, proclaiming myself to be a self-made ruler instead rightfully honoring God alone as the only King of all kings

- Wanting to be the center of the universe and having everyone look and pay attention to me, instead of praising, honoring, and giving glory to God, the only wise and true King of kings

- Trading all that we own and cherish—including parents, siblings, spouse, and children—in order to receive earthly riches, praise, and adoration

- Sacrificing my children for riches and promotion and leaving them emotionally starved of parental leadership, protective boundaries, hugs, cuddles, and affection that only a parent's love can supply to them

- Passing negative pronouncements, shame, and curses on family and others instead of blessing them
- Coming into agreement with the curses and lies of the enemy spoken over me and my family by ungodly leaders and wolves in sheep's clothing
- Receiving my identity from man and what others think of me instead of from You
- Seeing only myself, my needs, and my wants instead of seeing God and the needs of others
- Lavishly adorning myself while not covering the naked and caring for the homeless
- Not guarding my heart or rightly discerning my emotions and responding in the soul rather than in the spirit
- Not asking You to seal and protect me and to close off entrances to the enemy
- Not honoring Your wisdom, Your creation, Your design at an atomic and subatomic level, so that Your glory could come forth and Your light could be seen through me before conception and up until now
- Not correctly stewarding God's creation and having Godly dominion over the earth instead of greedily abusing God's resources coming into agreement with the spirit of greed and worshiping mammon instead of You
- Desiring the power and control that money brings and not submitting to Your control
- Desiring Your blessings, but not wanting to position myself in You to be blessed and a blessing to others
- The greed of my ancestors that gave away my inheritance; their lies, avarice greed, and for stealing from future generations
- Illegal trading of future generation's inheritance and blessing for immediate gratification, not having faith in the King of kings to

provide

- Loving money more than You, and clinging to the things of this world

Lord, please break all consequences of these sins; remove all curses, shame, and victimization; be King over all that I think and feel; cancel obligations that my ancestors put on me to pay back what is owed for future trading in the past. I appeal to Your justice and Your bloodshed on the cross, and ask You to declare in Your heavenly court that the ungodly agreements are illegal, null, and void.

I break agreements with the love of money, and let go of the things of this world.

Please cut off all ungodly strings to wealth.

I pledge my love to You, Jehovah Jireh, and look to You for provision. I declare that You are the Great I Am; the source of all that I have, all that I am, and all that I am to become. You are my Lord and my Redeemer.

I pray the prayer of Abraham Lincoln:

We have forgotten You, Lord. We have forgotten the gracious hand, which preserved us in peace and multiplied and enriched and strengthened us, and we have vainly imagined, in the deceitfulness of our hearts, that all these blessings were produced by some superior wisdom and virtue of our own. Intoxicated with unbroken success, we have become too self-sufficient to feel the necessity of redeeming and preserving grace, too proud to pray to the God that made us.

I repent for pride, self-sufficiency, and not giving thanks for Your abundant blessings.

I repent for valuing time and my schedule more than you, for loving time and the control of time, 'me' time, my time and quality time, instead of getting into Your time and asking You to order my day according to Your desire. Please forgive me for allowing time to control me and not seeking You first and for not seeking Your rest and restoration. Lord, please release me from any ungodly time warps or places where I've been stuck in time. Please reestablish my generational timeline according to Your Kairos timeline and reconcile me to your correct Kairos timeline. Please remove me from any ungodly timeline from the enemy in the depth; purify my time with your living water; wash away all the old timelines. Please align my inner clock to synchronize with Your heartbeat, sound, and movement.

Lord, please cleanse the elements of my physical body and the body of Christ. I declare that I will be a living stone, properly fitted together in the Body of Christ in timeless eternity with You.

Lord, please return to my DNA all components that were given away or stolen from my generational line; correctly align the order and sequence of all the components of my DNA; restore the health, wealth, blessing, and favor that should be inherent in my DNA structure; reverse the curse on my DNA when Adam sinned, and return to me the original blessing that was designed in my family's DNA; and release all the inherent blessings that were given to my family's DNA.

Lord, please release the components of my DNA that were trapped by stealing, illegal trading, and giving away by my ancestors in exchange for instant gratification from the enemy. Please reestablish both the vibration of the electrons that connect the elemental parts of my DNA and the correct frequency and vibration to the chemical bonds in my DNA.

I declare that all the earth belongs to You. Please remove me from ungodly places in the heavens, the depth, the length, the width, and the height, and reestablish the correct grid on the earth, above the earth, and under the earth.

Lord, please unearth the treasures of darkness stolen from my generational line and from the kingdom of God, and remove the ungodly guardians over the ungodly places in the depths that hold back what belongs to me and to Your kingdom. I declare that all I have and all that is owed to me belong to You to Your kingdom.

Lord, I appeal to Your written word and to the spiritual laws that You have set up in Your kingdom—Your kingdom laws. Where the King's law rules, there will be a year of Jubilee; and since You honored that law thousands of years ago, I declare there have been multiple jubilees, and I lay claim for all of them, declaring that today is my Day of Jubilee. I declare that all ungodly trading by my ancestors and the debt that I have been paying to be null and void; it is cancelled and is no more. I ask for a seven-fold return at current market price for all that has been lost, stolen, or given away in my generational line.

Lord, I anticipate through faith and declare that my trading will now be done in faith. My trust is in you Lord, and I trade by faith and say You have my life. I trust in You, and thank You that it will be accomplished according to Your time.

Lord, I present this prayer in the heavenly court as the prayer of my heart. I ask You to appropriate this prayer to my personal life; I ask for Your justice; I ask that this prayer be entered into Your courts as a legal document. Jesus, as my Advocate, I ask that You go before the Father, and ask the Father to declare this a 'done deal' in my life and in my generational line.

CHAPTER EIGHTEEN
LIFE CHANGING EVENTS ALONG THE WAY

The Lord often speaks to me through dreams, and the revelation of the Morning Star began with one. One night I (Paul) dreamt that I was getting off one bus and transferring to another, knowing that I still had a third one to go. Boarding the second bus and sitting right behind the driver's seat, I realized that I had left my computer case and baggage on the previous bus. We were on our way to Santa Fe Springs, California.

The day after the dream, I was going to Las Vegas for a one-day marketplace ministry. It was the first time in my life that I can remember flying without any baggage (and I now have 2,200,000 miles on American Airlines). While traveling to the airport, I phoned Barbara Parker and asked her to find out what Santa Fe Springs means. She looked up the name of the city and called me right back; and I was astounded to learn that Santa Fe Springs means Holy Faith Springs. I was on my way to holy faith, which needs to spring up. Then she said, "You are only beginning the second part of three parts of your life," and I thought, "Lord, I am already so tired." But I knew we were about to go in a new direction.

I was an American Baptist pastor. I had grown up as a Southern Baptist and became an American Baptist in college. I eventually went on staff at the church, went back to seminary, became a pastor, and then pastored for twenty years. You could say my life was simply routine until Saturday, October 7, 1989, at 1:00 P.M., when the Lord surprised me during a prayer session and, following His leading, I performed my first deliverance without knowing what I was doing. *Ravens* is the book that I wrote is about that experience. For me, it was a life-changing day, and my life has never been the same since. But this was just the first life changing experience; there was more to come.

The second life-changing event occurred in August 1991 when, for the first time, I started feeling pressure on my head. The Lord started teaching me about discerning demons; then angels, and then a host of other spiritual beings that are described in *Spiritual Servants of the Most High God*.

In May 2009, I took another leap of faith that became a third life-changing event. On the first Sunday of the month I was conducting a weekend school with a group of about fourteen. My wife, Donna, had been suffering terribly with pain from a shoulder injury so I conducted the school at our house so I wouldn't have to leave her alone. All of a sudden, someone saw a picture of the Mayan calendar. We began asking the Lord why He wanted us to focus on this. The Lord told us that the Mayans had spiritually affected the land of Hesperia[1] where we lived.

Our three-year-old house was situated on land that had never been developed before, and there was something key about that. As we waited on the Lord, He said, "You need to clean off the land." So we gathered together and simply said a very profound prayer, "Lord, clean the land off." Immediately I started feeling witchcraft coming off the land; it was a massive deliverance and we were all very shocked. I had lived in that house for three years, but I had never discerned this level of witchcraft. I could feel it coming off the land for over an hour. Suddenly, there was a spiritual shift and I experienced the manifestation of a new spiritual being. It was only later that I understood I was discerning a being called a star or the morning star. Sometime later I also discovered that Hesperia means, 'Star in the West'.

For many days afterward, the being manifested so powerfully on my head that I could hardly sleep at night because my entire left side was burning and felt like it was covered with hot weights. With the pressure there was also an awareness of a sensation of something like Fourth of July sparklers radiating off my body.

When I first started in deliverance ministry, I was told that one day I would say a word and the enemy would be cast out, unaware at the time that this is what Jesus did. Some years later, a friend from Alaska called me and said, "I got this passage for you—Matthew 8:16." I went to that verse and was amazed to find that it was about how, with one word, Jesus cast out evil. My friend asked if I knew what the verse meant and I replied, "I think I do." So I tried it; I said a word, and all of a sudden I would lock into the person and would feel the deliverance coming off of him.

Since discerning the star, my life has radically changed. Often, as the Lord was training me, I would sometimes war for hours or days against the demonic realm. Now, with the revelation of the star, there is tremendous power.

The star seems to manifest in two different ways, either radiating out like a sparkler or becoming like a black hole that sucks in evil. Deliverance occurs rapidly, so fast that nothing can stand against the power of the star. At some level this star seems to become a black hole from which no evil can escape. This is the power that the Lord is now unleashing on the earth for deliverance and for freedom.

[1] Hesperia, California, is on the road between Los Angeles and Las Vegas. To get there you travel up from the LA Basin and over the Cajon Pass, arriving in the High Desert at about 3,000 feet. It is on what is known as the Mormon Trail, which is the trail from Salt Lake to San Bernardino. It is also a place where a lot of horse thievery took place over the years.

CHAPTER NINETEEN
REVELATION OF THE MORNING STAR

What are these stars? As a Baptist pastor I (Paul) had taught that one-third of the stars fell and that they were angels. As I have mentioned before, the Lord is showing us that the Bible means what it says and not what we say it means. Stars are not angels but another kind of spiritual being. The Bible speaks often of stars.

Job 38:4-7 relates the beginning of the Lord's response to Job's contention about his suffering:

> *Where were you when I laid the foundations of the earth? Tell Me, if you have understanding. Who determined its measurements? Surely you know! Or who stretched the line upon it? To what were its foundations fastened? Or who laid its cornerstone, When the morning stars sang together, And all the sons of God shouted for joy?*

Some commentators speculate 'sons of God and stars' are phrases that are examples of Hebrew parallelism; a method used to explain the way a Hebrew would state a word or phrase in one way and then express it in another way. According to this teaching, 'morning stars' would be repeated in another way as 'sons of God'. Others have taught the stars were simply a description of angels. As the Lord allowed us to experience a star as a separate kind of spiritual being, we realized we were not sensing angels but stars. It also became apparent that we all seemed to have at least one star assigned to us.

Sometime after the beginning of this revelation I was troubled by a passage in Revelation 1:20:

> *The mystery of the seven stars which you saw in My right hand, and the seven golden lampstands: The seven stars are the angels of the seven churches, and the seven lampstands which you saw are the seven churches.*

The New King James Version clearly says the stars are the angels. If the new revelation was true, how could this be? So I looked up the Greek word for angels. *Angelos* is the Greek word for angels, but it is also correctly translated 'messenger'. For example, in Matthew 11:10, John the Baptist is called an *angelos* or messenger, yet it is clear he is not an angel. Therefore, I would believe that the correct translation of Revelation would be, "The mystery of the seven stars which you saw in My right hand, and the seven golden lampstands: The seven stars are the <u>messengers</u> of the seven churches, and the seven lampstands which you saw are the seven churches."

These stars seem to be very powerful, and according to scripture war for us. Judges 5:19-20 illustrates this truth:

> *The kings came and fought, Then the kings of Canaan fought in Taanach, by the waters of Megiddo; They took no spoils of silver. They fought from the heavens; The stars from their courses fought against Sisera.*

Now, let's look at Revelation 2:18-28.

> *And to the angel of the church in Thyatira write, "These things says the Son of God, who has eyes like a flame of fire, and His feet like fine brass: I know your works, love, service, faith and your patience; and as for your works, the last are more than the first. Nevertheless I have a few things against you, because you allow that woman Jezebel, who calls herself a prophetess, to teach and seduce My servants to commit sexual immorality and eat things sacrificed to idols. And I gave her time to repent of her sexual immorality, and she did not repent. Indeed I will cast her into a sickbed, and those who commit adultery with her into great tribulation, unless they repent of their deeds. I will kill her children with death, and all the churches shall know that I am He who searches the minds and hearts. And I will give to each one of you according to your works. Now to you I say, and to the rest in Thyatira, as many as do not have this doctrine, who has not known the depths of Satan, as they say, I will put on you no other burden. But hold fast what you have till I come. And he who overcomes, and keeps My works until the end, to him I will give power over the nations—He shall rule them with a rod of iron; They shall be dashed to pieces like the potter's vessels—as I also have received*

from My Father; and I will give him the morning star."

As I was researching the concept of the star being a spiritual entity, I told some that as I was praying for people I would feel the deliverance as if pottery was shattering. Imagine my surprise when, after the revelation of the star, I discovered that last phrase:

> *'They shall be dashed to pieces like the potter's vessels'—as I also have received from My Father; and I will give him the morning star.*

This warring is very aggressive and effective, and seems to result in the shattering of the plans of the enemy. The word translated 'nations' is really the Greek word 'ethos', meaning 'peoples'. I saw that and I was shocked. I realized that the power the Lord is now releasing on His church is power over the peoples in the generational line. He is breaking apart the evil in the generational line like a piece of pottery. He is shattering that evil in our family line, destroying it, and sucking it into a black hole so that we can live in freedom. Here is more evidence of the power of the stars and how they are tied to our position in Christ.

CHAPTER 20

THE STAR AND THE BODY OF CHRIST

Very early in my (Paul) deliverance ministry the Lord taught me to discern the pentagram on people. I could feel the five hot spots on their body. After the revelation of the star, I realized that the pentagram is simply a perversion of the star. When I first started discerning the star, I realized that I could feel a burning sensation on my feet, my hands, and my forehead. The power of God was so strong on me.

On that Sunday afternoon I also realized that I could feel seven hot spots on a person's body. It was then I realized that I was discerning the seven spots called charka points by those in Hinduism and the New Age movement. These hot spots are on the forehead, mouth, neck, heart, solar plexus, genitals, and the head.

I started asking the Lord to reveal the Biblical name for these points. After a period of time I was reminded of Zechariah 4:10:

> For who has despised the day of small things? For these seven rejoice to see The plumb line in the hand of Zerubbabel. They are the eyes of the LORD, Which scan to and fro throughout the whole earth.

Now compare the Zechariah passage to Revelation 5:6:

> And I looked and behold, in the midst of the throne and of the four living creatures, and in the midst of the elders, stood a Lamb as though it had been slain, having seven horns and seven eyes, which are the seven Spirits of God sent out into all the earth.

It would suggest the seven eyes of the Lamb are these seven 'power points' on the body. These seven points are tied somehow to the seven spirits of God.[1]

I was surprised as I was discerning these hot spots for one woman when, all of a sudden, I felt that the hot spot moved over to her heart. I thought, "Lord, why did the hot spot move to the heart?" Eventually I felt the heat move back to the center of the body by the heart. A person then remembered the scripture in 2 Peter 1:19:

And so we have the prophetic word confirmed, which you do well to heed as a light that shines in a dark place, until the day dawns and the morning star rises in your hearts.

Just after the event in May, one of our intercessors said, "Since the Lord released that star to us, that star has now gone out on lines and it is touching everybody that you have prayed for." There is more to understand about the eyes of the Lord, but it seems that we are connected to other believers by the eyes of the Lord.

A couple of days later, my son called and he was with a youth group out in the desert. They had a telescope and they wanted to look at the stars. He said, "Dad, it is really windy. Would you just pray that the wind stops?" We got together and said, "Lord, would You stop the wind?" And the wind stopped. Never in all of my life have I seen such an immediate answer to prayer. I wondered if somehow there is power tied to the eyes of the Lord.

Next, a friend of mine, the very friend that I had gone to be with in Las Vegas, called me and said, "Paul, I need to tell you that I have a good friend who is a quadriplegic. I went to his house and I prayed for him and all of a sudden he lifted his foot four inches." We have seen amazing answers to prayer since the revelation of the star. Now look at Psalm 16:1-6:

Preserve me O God, for in You I put my trust. O my soul, you have said to the LORD, "You are my LORD, My goodness is nothing apart from You." As for the saints who are on the earth, "They are the excellent ones in whom is all my delight." Their sorrows shall be multiplied who hasten after another god; Their drink offerings of blood I will not offer, Nor take up their names on my lips. O LORD, You are the portion of my inheritance and my cup; You maintain my lot. The lines have fallen to me in pleasant places; Yes, I have a good inheritance.

The week before the revelation of the star, a lady came to our weekend school on Sunday. She had not been there on Saturday and when she arrived, I said, "You were supposed to be here today weren't you?" She said, "Yes, the Lord told me to come." When she walked in, I suddenly discerned astral projection, which is a practice of cults and New Agers. (They actually travel with their soul to other places. Those who have experienced it say that they can feel their silver cord, which is a spiritual cord that I can feel that is tied to the belly button.) I looked at her and I said, "You have all these lines coming out of your neck. It is like people are astral projecting through your neck, as if you are stuck in some ungodly place and astral projection is actually traveling on these lines through you." She asked, "What will we do?" I said, "Well, I guess we better get you out of there," so we prayed and asked the Lord to remove her from this ungodly place.

Later, after the revelation of the star, somehow we came to Song of Solomon 4:4, *Your neck is like the tower of David, Built for an armory, On which hang a thousand bucklers* (or a thousand shields), so I went up to somebody and checked to see what could be discerned, and I could feel all these lines coming off of that person's neck. There is something significant about how *the lines have fallen to me in pleasant places*[2] relates to these bucklers. The Shulamite woman in Song of Solomon symbolizes the Church, and Solomon symbolizes Jesus as the Bridegroom. The Shulamite woman is the Bride. As the Bride, you have all these lines coming off you and somehow these are tied to the star.

The revelation of the star and the stars is in the infant stage. The next books in the *Exploring Heavenly Realms* will discuss our growth in the wisdom of the Lord about the stars.

[1] Isaiah 11:2
[2] Psalm 16:6

108

CHAPTER TWENTY-ONE
PRAYER TO RELEASE THE MORNING STAR

Father God, I repent for myself and my ancestors for allowing my light to become dull, preventing me from allowing Your glory to shine through me. Forgive me for not becoming a partaker of the divine nature of Christ, allowing instead the corruption of the world to dull the reflection of Christ within me.

Lord, thank You for being light, and that no darkness at all dwells in You. I repent for claiming to have fellowship with You, yet walking in darkness; lying and not practicing the truth; and being blinded by the light. Holy Spirit, teach me to walk in the Light of my Lord Jesus. Father God, cleanse me by the blood of Jesus from all sin so that I may have fellowship with You and the Body of Christ.

I repent for claiming to know You but not keeping Your commandments; for hating my brother, yet not helping him in his time of need and closing my heart against him.

Teach me to love in deed and in truth so that I may abide in the light. Remove the darkness that has blinded my eyes.

I renounce the love of the world and the things of the world keeping out the love of the Father. I repent for the lust of the flesh, the lust of the eyes, and the boastful pride of life. I choose to do the will of the Father, and pray for discernment to not be deceived in these last days by the spirit of antichrist. Holy Spirit, I ask for a revelation of truth that I may practice righteousness, abide in Your light, and not be deceived.

I repent for holding to the letter of the law instead of embracing the Spirit. Let my faith be dependent upon the demonstration of the Spirit and His power rather than on human wisdom. Let the wisdom of God be revealed within me by the Spirit of God so that I might know Him.

I repent for practicing sin, lawlessness, and deceit. Holy Spirit, as a child of God, please teach me to keep my eyes fixed on You that I may become pure; an imitator of my Lord Jesus.

Father God, Your word says that You are a jealous God and I am to have no other gods before You. I repent of entering into idolatry by:

- Forsaking Your commands
- Making idols
- Making Asherah poles
- Bowing down to the starry hosts
- Worshiping Baal
- Erecting alters to Baal
- Building altars to all the starry hosts in both courts of the Lord's temple
- Consulting mediums and spiritists
- Sacrificing our sons and daughters in the fire
- Practicing divination and sorcery
- Telling ourselves to do evil in Your eyes, and provoking You to anger
- Swearing by Molech
- Turning back from following You, neither seeking nor inquiring of You
- Practicing violence and deceit
- Following the ways of the enemy by seeking to ascend to heaven, building my own kingdom, raising my throne above the stars of God, seeking to sit enthroned on the mount of assembly on the utmost heights of the sacred mountain, ascending above the tops of the clouds, and seeking to make myself like the Most High

Lord, please break off the consequences of these sins—isolation from You, affliction, effects of being plundered, removal from Your presence, wandering from the land you gave my forefathers, lawlessness, and fighting between fathers and sons.

Father God, I repent for not showing and seeking goodness; not seeking righteous knowledge; not demonstrating self-control or perseverance; and not exhibiting godliness, brotherly kindness, or love. Please break off the consequences of ineffectiveness, nearsightedness, blindness, and unproductiveness in my knowledge of Jesus Christ.

Father, thank You that every good and perfect gift is from above, coming down from You, the Father of the heavenly lights; that You do not change like shifting shadows; and that the morning stars sang together and all the heavenly beings shouted for joy.

I repent for:

- Worshiping heavenly bodies, hosts, stars, and planets; especially Venus who is called the Morning Star
- Wishing on stars
- Making decisions by stars
- Trying to read the times by stars
- Worshiping stars
- Practicing astrology
- Tolerating Jezebel
- Committing adultery with Jezebel
- Holding to her teaching
- Embracing Satan's so-called deep secrets

Father, remove from me the intense suffering and the consequences of coming into agreement with and tolerating Jezebel. Lord Jesus, teach me to hold on to what I have until Your return. In overcoming Jezebel, I will receive authority over the nations, to rule them with an iron scepter and to dash them to pieces like pottery, just as You received authority from Your Father; and I will receive You, the Morning Star. Give me ears to hear what You, Spirit of God, say to Your church.

I repent for having and being the light of the world, yet hiding that light under a bushel. Forgive me for not letting my light shine before men, so they may see my good works and glorify my Father in heaven.

Father God, thank you that Your divine power has given me everything I need for life and godliness through my knowledge of You; thank You for calling me by Your own glory and goodness. You have given me Your very great and precious promises, through which I may participate in the divine nature and escape the corruption in the world caused by evil desires.

Father God, please teach and empower me to add:

- To my faith, goodness
- To goodness, knowledge
- To knowledge, self-control
- To self-control, perseverance
- To perseverance, godliness
- To godliness, brotherly kindness
- To brotherly kindness, love

I declare that if I possess these qualities in increasing measure, they will keep me from being ineffective and unproductive in my knowledge of You. If I do these things, I will never fall.

Father, thank You for giving me Your Word through the prophets, and teach me to pay attention to it as to a light shining in a dark place until the day dawns and the morning star rises in my heart. Lord restore to me Your presence, and raise the morning star in my heart.

I repent for coming into agreement with the enemy and accepting the enemy's ungodly covering that hides the light of the Lord. Please remove ungodly coverings, brandings, and fire from me. I renounce all agreements with the enemy, and I ask You to remove the dark gauze and shadow placed over me, which keep Your light from shining in my being. Burn away the darkness and corruption with Your fire and Your light.

I repent for allowing a veil of unbelief and doubt to overcome me.

Lord, please remove veils from my heart that keep me from understanding and receiving Your truth, and from shining Your light before men.

Lord, please lift off the garment of heaviness and replace it with a garment of praise; lift off mourning and replace it with Your oil of joy; lift off ashes and dashed hopes, and replace them with beauty. Therefore, I will be called an oak of righteousness, displaying the splendor and light of the Lord.

Lord, in place of the ungodly covering, please cover me with Your feathers and hide me under the shelter of Your wings that I might find refuge.

Lord, please:

- Remove the veil that lies on my heart, keeping me from receiving Your truth
- Remove the veil that covers Your light and glory that shines through me
- Remove all ungodly vibrations, sounds, numbers, sequences and lights of the enemy; and redeem of all that the enemy has stolen from my family line and grant a seven-fold return
- Redeem, adjust and align the music, equations, colors, lights, vibrations and DNA that the enemy has tampered with and used for his purposes

I repent for building ungodly structures such as the tower of Babel, pyramids, ziggurats, high places, pinnacles, temples, and Stonehenge in order to become like God; for building their kingdom and worshiping the heavenly hosts. I repent for ungodly alignment with the stars and planets. Please tear down the ungodly structures and build Your Godly structures on the cornerstone of Jesus Christ and the foundation of the apostles and prophets.

Lord, please disconnect me from the ungodly structures and land de led by my ancestors. Cleanse me from walking on defiled land, and decontaminate the multidimensional ley lines to reestablish Your highways of holiness.

I repent for elevating celebrities, ministers, worship leaders, politicians, and movie stars to idol status; and for worshiping them as stars and heroes. Lord, forgive me for drawing from people in ungodly dependence, and I release them to You. I also forgive those drawing from me, and I break ungodly connections that have been placed upon me to drain my energy and anointing. Forgive me for drawing my identity from others instead of seeking and finding my identity in You, as a son of God with privileges of a son.

Lord, please remove and disconnect me from ungodly dimensions, wormholes, portals; including time portals and time dimensions that enable me to build the enemy's kingdom. Please disconnect me from ungodly stones and structures building the enemy's kingdom, and bring alignment to ungodly magnetic fields. I repent for embracing the Age of Aquarius that opened the door to star and planet worship and to the new age.

Lord, please align and reconfigure my body, soul, and spirit to Your sound, colors, vibrations, frequencies, and notes that create matter and destroy impurities. Adjust the elements in my physical body and brain to function as You created them to function at creation, and remove all defilement from the elements in the land to which my ancestors and I have been connected. Please take me to Your heavenly places and remove all defilement from the land and me.

I repent for allowing the enemy to take over the airways and sending into the atmosphere negative sound waves through words of discord, negative speech, and gossip; and for not coming into unity in one accord. I repent for playing and listening to ungodly music containing negative speech and profanity. Forgive me for speaking and tolerating profanity.

I repent for releasing sounds into the atmosphere that empower negative forces and foreign gods; for watching movies and television programs influenced by the spirit of the antichrist; for passing on corrupt communication by allowing the transmission of information to pass through the atmosphere and the ground through frequencies and signals from computers, iPods, iPhones, iTunes, YouTube, Facebook, and other means. Lord, please dismantle the control stations of the airwaves that have been empowered by negativity and ungodly sounds released into the air; and redeem the airwaves so that Godly, life releasing sounds can be transmitted.

Lord Jesus, You are the Root and the Offspring of David, the Bright and Morning Star. I keep my eyes on You, so that I may be a reflection of Your light and beauty. Shine Your light in me and through me so there will not be any darkness in or around me, and so You may be magnified and glorified.

CHAPTER TWENTY-TWO
ONGOING REVELATION OF THE HEIGHT, WIDTH, AND LENGTH

'The unexpected is unexpected', a cliché, but nevertheless true. As a pastor I (Paul) would study the scripture, carefully examining the words, phrases, and sentences; and understanding would eventually come. It is no longer like that because the Lord, in His kindness, has now taken us on a different kind of journey; a journey that has unlocked scripture in ways I never dreamed possible. The unexpected has happened.

As I minister alongside other believers, we often confront difficult issues of spiritual, mental and physical health. Determined to understand what is happening, we ask the Lord for help and revelation comes. Suddenly, we are driven back to familiar scriptures and words, but they now explode to reveal new, never-before-apparent insights. Application of these newly realized truths results in new levels of healing.

The year 2010 was a year of accelerated revelation. It was the year when three words—width, length, and height—moved from being components of verse to concepts impregnated with thoughts so vast as to cause us to wonder at the complexities of the creation of God. We are now convinced that this is just the beginning of our understanding, and what the Lord has yet to show us about these regions is really beyond our imagination.

In May 2010, I was in Manhattan doing ministry with another prayer minister when an angel came with a message, and the unexpected happened:

> This is a spiritual being called 'the height'. You must go down to go up. As it was said from glory to glory, the revelation unfolds. Since you have been faithful with the little, I will give you the more. Your fulfillment is in hope. Your desire emanates in delight. Desire makes the way; it

opens the way because it is connected to faith—hope, desire, and faith. The seven [spirits of God] all hold the key for the next level to be received. Learn well from this journey; it is a new journey; I will multiply it.

In this place you take dominion; each level is a position received; each level is a position redeemed, dethroned, and enthroned. Perception is changed. You will learn true ruling, true reigning:

Every level carries manifold wisdom; wisdom is justified by her children. There is a multiplication of endowment of wisdom at every level; she has hewn out her seven pillars. If the Lord does not build the house, they labor in vain. It is more expansive than compartmentalized; you take dominion on each level. At every door and every gate, wisdom cries out. Every pathway, where the paths meet, you create a path, a new one; you take position by decision, by declaration, by agreement. Every level will hold the decision and an edict will be set; it is the new law for every level by the order of Melchizedek. At one hand the old is done away with; at one hand the new law comes; at one hand the old covenant is done away with; at the other hand a new covenant. Every time something is agreed upon it is written down and decreed. A level dispensation follows. There is more to come, but not for now, until you reach the 8.

It was then I understood that the height is a place of ruling and reigning. But what does it mean to say it is a place? Is it a region? A collection of dimensions? A realm? Ephesians 3:18 mentions *width, length, height, and depth*. Are these quadrants or coordinates? Seemingly, new revelation only begets new questions! And then I pondered, "What did it mean, 'Until you reach the 8'"?

Then came August 8, 2013. I was praying with a woman who had left a very controlling husband. In reality, she had been lost in the sphere of her husband, a man who had defined her identity to the point that she had not moved into the fullness of the call on her life.

Having felt that she was to be with me in ministry that day, the prayer minister who had also been in Manhattan was present. Unexpectedly, the unexpected happened again. Prompted by the Spirit, I rediscovered the word from 2010 with the mention of '8', realized it was now 8/8, and we became aware that we were in the Godly height. The Lord revealed more about the height as a new word was delivered for the client.

A different kind of angel is here. It has a sound. These angels inhabit the Godly height:

The abundance of His great goodness abounded to produce the fruit of the land in abundance and to bear the truth. But these [members of the generational line] would not have it; they abused the gifts, so they destroyed it and buried it in desolation and guilt. Hope was destroyed by what they didn't receive, and did they not honor the gift Giver for they honored and believed in themselves. [This sin placed the generational line into the ungodly height]

You tried and it hasn't worked. You are not the sacrifice. You are not the burden bearer. You are the gift that is given to reveal the truth. And you have been walking so long that nobody hears from a place of isolation. You agreed in fear. He [the husband] could not go where you are going so he took you to where he is. You are not alone, but you have a key.

The Lord showed us that generational sins had enabled ungodly rule in the past to be knitted into the lady, placing her in the ungodly height. Instead of ruling and reigning with Christ, she had become a slave to the enemy and to her husband, subjugated to being the tail instead of being the head. Instead of ruling and reigning over creation with her husband, she remained a player in the drama created by the husband; and he had become the center of her universe rather than the Lord. Through prayer, she confessed the generational sin and asked the Lord to remove her from the ungodly height and place her into her rightful position of ruling and reigning.

Even as we were receiving our initial information about the depth and height, I began to wonder if the Lord would also reveal characteristics of the length and width. I did not have to wait long. In July 2010, while praying for a client, the Lord gave us the first glimpse of the width. I remember it so clearly because I had become very discouraged. Two months earlier our city had sent a letter stating that we had to cease ministry in our location; and now, not only had our efforts to overturn the decision failed, but we had also been unsuccessful in finding a new location. I was determined to have faith for the future, but my emotions would not cooperate with my faith. This day, the Lord revealed that the client was stuck in an ungodly place under a false tabernacle; an unstable location that rotated among the stars so that one could never feel established; a place where doubt and unbelief ruled to such an extent that there would be murmuring and complaining; a place where God would not respond to any need. As we prayed, the Lord instructed us to ask Him to remove the client from this ungodly width. I joined in the prayer for myself, and was totally shocked by what transpired next! Suddenly the doubt and despair lifted off and instantly, I experienced faith. The change was permanent.

The following weeks would reveal that the width is a place of the heart; a place where faith, hope, and love abide. If past generations have ignored the Lord, or if our lives have not been correctly centered in the Lord, then we have been set up to dwell in the ungodly width, and our hearts have grown weary. To live in the righteous width is to experience the joy of the Father, and we are just scratching the surface of its complexities. Further books will explore the wonders of this place.

The following year, in June 2011, the Lord surprised us at an intern meeting in Collingwood, Canada, with the initial revelation about the length. He showed us that the righteous length is a place of unity and oneness, including sexual unity; and the ungodly length is a place where we are incorrectly tied to others. We will continue to explore this region of our humanness in order to reveal how it is possible to experience new levels of freedom that we never knew were possible.

We expect much more to come in future volumes of *Exploring Heavenly Places*.